FOR MARY RIVES BOWMAN

who shared a journey to Troy
and the ascent of Thera's zigzag trail,
two of many adventures in travel.

μουσικὴν ποίει καὶ ἐργάζου

. . . 'make music and work at it.'

—Plato

Marjorie Braymer

ATLANTIS

THE BIOGRAPHY OF A LEGEND

A Margaret K. McElderry Book

ATHENEUM 1983 NEW YORK

LIBRARY OF CONGRESS CATALOGING IN PUBLICATION DATA

BRAYMER, MARJORIE.
ATLANTIS, THE BIOGRAPHY OF A LEGEND.
"A MARGARET K. MCELDERRY BOOK."
BIBLIOGRAPHY: P. 217
SUMMARY: EXAMINES THE LEGENDS OF SEVERAL
CENTURIES CONCERNING THE EXISTENCE OF ATLANTIS
AND DESCRIBES THE RECENT DISCOVERY OF RUINS ON AN
ISLAND IN THE AEGEAN SEA WHICH CLOSELY RESEMBLE
PLATO'S DESCRIPTION OF THE LOST ISLAND.
1. ATLANTIS—JUVENILE LITERATURE. [1 ATLANTIS]
I. TITLE.
GN751.B74 1983   398.2'34   82-16727
ISBN 0-689-50264-8

CONTENTS

ACKNOWLEDGMENTS

The author wishes to thank many persons whose help has been invaluable in the preparation of this book. Few requests for information went unanswered, whether addressed to authors, publishers, museums or libraries. It has been a gratifying experience.

Mr. and Mrs. M. H. L. Sanders, Jr., have generously allowed the publication of their New Map of the Terraqueous Globe.

Professor Thomas C. Gillmer has my gratitude for the use of his Thera ship drawing, which is reprinted with permission of *The Mariner's Mirror,* the Quarterly Journal of the Society for Nautical Research.

I must thank the Archaeological Society of Athens for the two site plans from *Excavations at Thera VII* by Spyridon Marinatos.

The seventeenth-century Dutch map of Atlantis is used by permission of the Mansell Collection.

Photographs of pages from the Dresden Codex are reproduced by courtesy of the Sächsische Landesbibliothek, Dresden.

The University of Oklahoma Press has my thanks for permission to reprint drawings from *Incidents of Travel in Yucatán* by John Lloyd Stephens, new edition copyright 1962.

Spiro Meletzis has kindly provided the photograph of Dr. Marinatos.

The Danish Museum of Copenhagen has given permission to reproduce the photo of the inlaid bronze dagger blade from Thera.

Joseph J. Bonsignore, publisher of *Smithsonian,* has my cordial thanks for making it possible to reproduce pictures of the first Thera frescoes. The photographs are by Dmitri Kessel.

Mary Alice Kier's pictures of the excavation site at Thera were taken in 1974, and are previously unpublished. I feel privileged to present these studies of the excavation then in full progress.

The photo of the great shed at Akrotiri is by Chris Shutes and adds a further dimension to the extent of the site.

Mary A. Cowden has my thanks for the use of her photograph of the zigzag donkey trail as seen from the caldera with the town of Phirá above.

The magazine *Antiquity* readily gave permission to use several quotations from the 1939 article by Dr. Marinatos.

Oxford University Press has consented to my quoting from the poem "Atlantis" in *Collected Poems by Conrad Aiken, 1953.*

Little, Brown and Company has granted permission to publish an excerpt from Emily Dickinson's poem "I dwell in Possibility—" from *The Complete Poems of Emily Dickinson,* copyright 1929, © 1957 by Mary R. Hampson.

I am indebted to L. J. Mellick for the diagrams of Atlantis as Plato describes it. They catch the spirit of his words and are drawn to scale.

The plans of the House of Frescoes, and the Severed House, both drawn by Mamet, were adapted from *Santorin et ses éruptions* by Ferdinand Fouqué, edited by G. Masson, Libraire de l'Académe de Medecine, Paris, 1879.

From Marjorie Robineau Kohn I have learned that a fine librarian is also part magician. She found materials that seemed unobtainable or lost in dusty archives. I am most grateful not only for these efforts but for valuable suggestions she offered as the book progressed.

Gerald Goff came gallantly to my rescue with translations from some academic Latin and technical French.

From the start of this work to its finish, Jeanne Maurer Shutes has given creative suggestions and encouragement. So doing, she has helped to *believe* it into being.

To Margaret K. McElderry I must express deep gratitude for her sensitive editing.

FOREWORD

What is a legend? More often than not, it is an ancient story that may be rooted in an actual historic event. Its historical accuracy cannot be proved, but neither can it be disproved. It has been around so long and repeated so frequently that "the memory of man runneth not to the contrary." A legend is a *could-have-been,* a *may-be.*

A little more than a century ago the legendary city of Troy was said to be impossible to find, a dream city created by Homer. But look what happened to Troy! In 1873, the archaeologist Heinrich Schliemann discovered its ruins. The story of King Arthur and his knights is called a legend. More recently, there have been excavations at Cadbury Hill, in southwest England, that turned up traces of a palace-fortress that might have been Arthur's home, Camelot.

One of the world's oldest legends, that of the lost island of Atlantis, has collided with living history. This book will trace its remarkable career from the remote past to the present day. It is a story filled with *may-be's* and *could-have-been's* that now can be considered in the light of known historical facts and some recent history-making discoveries.

One fact is that lost Atlantis may no longer be lost. It just *may be.*

M.B.
Carmel, California
1981

The Legend that Refused to Die

The first person to write the story of Atlantis was Plato, the poet-philosopher and teacher of ancient Athens. According to Plato, whose work is dated more than three centuries before Christ, the mighty empire of Atlantis lay west of the Pillars of Hercules in the Atlantic Ocean. Larger than Asia Minor and Libya combined, Atlantis was an island the size of a continent.

Its powerful rulers once sent their armies to attack cities in Europe and Asia. Their goal was to conquer the Mediterranean world. The land now called Italy was gravely threatened. Libya fell before them and became captive. Greece and Egypt were braced for invasion.

It was the soldiers of ancient Athens who took the brunt of the attack, Plato tells us. With great courage and military skill, the Athenians led an alliance of Greeks, then fought on alone when the others deserted them. They finally brought the fighting men of Atlantis to their knees, saving themselves as well as the Egyptians from slavery.

Some time afterward, the heroic Athenians were killed in a sudden disaster. Earthquakes and floods overwhelmed Athens and swept them to their death. At the same time the island of Atlantis was struck by violent earthquakes. Within the space of one day and one night, so terrible were the floods that it was swallowed up by the sea and vanished. Nothing remained, not a trace, except for a churning, muddy wake that made the waters around it hazardous to ships for years. The city of Athens eventually recovered, but Atlantis became only a memory. It had disappeared from the face of the earth.

In briefest outline this is the story of Atlantis as told by Plato. It would be hard to single out another story that has excited as much argument as this has. One question has been whether Plato invented the tale or wrote in the belief that its events were historically true. Many think that it was his way, as a teacher, to make the point that fair-minded, moderate men can overcome the most aggressive enemy. But the question persisted. Was there ever a real Atlantis or wasn't there?

People have disagreed sharply about Atlantis. They still do.

Meanwhile, a legend came into being. Plato's story gave birth to the legend, which has any number of themes and variations. In one of its infinite variations the legend maintains that Atlantis exists as a beautiful, ruined city somewhere under the sea. What sea? The answers are legion. Choose any sea you like! Why "beautiful"? But everyone knows that Atlantis was incomparably beautiful! (Plato himself had said that.) And its people were scientific geniuses; they had mastered the secrets of atomic energy and knew the key to everlasting life. (Plato said nothing of the kind.)

There are Atlantis fans today who think that the elusive island is about to be rediscovered. Some believe that it has already been found and claim that they know exactly where it is.

There are true believers in the legend who are sure that Atlantis was located in Spain, or in Mongolia, in Palestine, Nigeria, the Netherlands, Brazil, Sweden, or Greenland, or Yucatán. That's only a sample of the list of localities.

The full list covers dozens more. Legend-believers have put Atlantis in just about every nook and cranny of the globe: in desert lands, on mountain peaks, and fathoms deep on some ocean floor.

Now and then in human history an extraordinary event has occurred, such as a frightful plague or a famine or flood, and the memory of it has never faded, even when no survivors were left to tell what actually took place. The memory endures. Word-of-mouth reports keep it alive and tradition makes it seem more credible as time goes on. This is what has happened in the case of Atlantis.

The *legend* of Atlantis is a thing separate and apart from Plato's story. It is actually an enormous collection of theories and guesses. Some of them reach into realms of magic and mysticism. Some have a science-fiction twist. Taken all together, they make up an impressively large body of beliefs and conjectures, a sturdy old legend that stubbornly refuses to die.

Certain versions of the legend say that there were a few refugees from Atlantis who made their way to Egypt and founded that civilization. In other versions the survivors turn up in Yucatán and build those amazing stone cities in the New World. The Atlanteans, as the inhabitants of Atlantis are called, are frequently represented as beings of such superior intelligence that they had achieved an advanced civilization before any other existed in the world.

It is one version or another of the *legend,* not Plato's story, that has changed the lives of a surprisingly large number of people over the course of centuries. The prospect of discovering traces of a brilliant lost civilization is a spur to the laziest imagination. The Atlantis legend holds out an implied promise that with the correct clues to the puzzle, the mystery can be solved. Along with that promise goes a subtle hint that fame and riches will reward the discoverer.

Now, late in the twentieth century, Atlantis has made front-page news in the world press. A group of eminent scientists, among them archaeologists, seismologists, and oceanographers, thinks that a city resembling the Atlantis Plato described has been found. They offer some persuasive evidence to show that in many respects the island under study corresponds to his descriptions of Atlantis. It took heavy damage from the shocks of ancient volcanic upheavals and tidal waves, as its scarred cliffs and shorelines clearly reveal. Peasants work its fields and vineyards today in spite of occasional earth tremors, for this is still a volcanic island.

It is located not in Greenland nor in the land of the

Maya. The scientists have turned the world's attention to a little island in the Aegean Sea.

Here it is that floors, walls, and sometimes the roofs of buildings made by a Bronze Age people have been uncovered. They are fragile in the extreme. Inside them are remnants of bright-hued frescoes and pieces of furniture. Workmen's tools have been discovered, along with cooking ware and finely wrought pottery. They are the handiwork of a vanished people, whose society was at least as old as that of the Sea Kings of Crete, those rulers of the Minoan era who built sumptuous palaces and were at their height fifteen centuries before Christ.

This discovery has been hailed as *the most important archaeological event since the discovery of Pompeii.* Like Pompeiian buildings, the structures must be excavated from the heavy layers of volcanic ash and pumice that buried them. But they are more deeply buried and much older.

The scientists' reports concern the island of Santorini, or Thera, which is its ancient name, in the Aegean Sea. By ship it is a day's distance from mainland Greece and it lies sixty miles north of Crete.

Has this startling find put an end to the arguments about Atlantis? Far from it. The ruined buildings do not satisfy the expectations of people who are waiting to hear that the ruins of a marble city have been discovered beneath the sea. Those who view Atlantis as "the cradle of civilization" are not at all impressed. Plato said that Atlantis was "outside" or to the west of the Strait of Gibraltar. Since Santorini does not lie in that direction, the legend-believers take Plato's statement as proof positive that the excavations at Santorini, or Thera, count for nothing.

Before the colorful life of the legend is investigated, it is reasonable to see exactly what Plato wrote about Atlantis.

The Unknown History

The story of Atlantis is told in two of Plato's dialogues,
the *Timaeus* and the *Critias*. In the first of these it is
briefly told, more fully in the other. Plato explains that it
was brought back from Egypt by Solon, who was known
as the wisest of Greek statesmen and who believed it was
authentic history. More than that, Solon had taken notes
about the story. He planned to make it the subject of an
epic poem, although he never did.

The Atlantis tale came to Solon's attention when he
was traveling in Egypt over a hundred and fifty years
earlier than Plato's time. At Saïs, a city on the Nile Delta,
he went to talk with the priests of the main temple. His
fame as a legislator and a poet made him cordially welcome. The Egyptians admired the Athenians and regarded
them as kinsmen, since they believed their goddess Neïth
to be the same deity the Greeks called Athena. She was

the patron and protector of Greece as well as Egypt.

Solon listened intently as the priests told him about the war Athens had fought against Atlantis. According to Egyptian temple records, it had raged nine thousand years ago. Yet Solon knew nothing about Atlantis or its aggressive war.

In the distant past, he was told, a confederation of powerful kings ruled the island of Atlantis and many other islands also. They launched the war from their homeland in the Atlantic Ocean by sending their forces to attack cities in Europe and Asia. The men of Athens led a coalition of all Greeks and halted it. Then, hard-pressed though they were when their allies deserted them, they fought on alone. They saved their own country from invasion and prevented Egypt from being overrun. Finally they generously freed other countries held captive by Atlantis. For these gallant actions the Egyptians were forever grateful to the Athenians.

Their enemy was totally defeated. Later on, violent earthquakes and floods overwhelmed the island of Atlantis and it disappeared into the sea. The fighting men of Athens were also swallowed up in a tremendous flood— all this in one day and night of horror.

Later in his story, Plato gives the history of Atlantis, as Solon heard it. Solon's written notes were handed down in his family. In the beginning of time, Plato tells, the immortal gods divided the world among themselves into portions each would rule. As his share Poseidon, lord of the sea and god of earthquakes, received Atlantis. It was an island larger than Libya and Asia together. He chose to marry a mortal woman, Cleito, and with her he founded the royal family of Atlantis.

He selected for Cleito's home a hill at the very center of the island. It overlooked a large fertile plain, one side of which was bordered by the sea.

For the protection of his beloved wife, Poseidon surrounded the hilltop home with five concentric rings of water and land. Two of them were of land and three were of sea water. He carved these "wheels" or rings with the effortless ease of a god, making an inner island of Cleito's home on the hill. In later years it became the city's acropolis. Poseidon commanded warm and cold springs to bubble from the earth. His descendants would never lack water for any purpose.

Cleito bore Poseidon ten sons—five sets of twin boys. Atlas was the first-born son of the oldest pair, and Poseidon made him king. His brothers were appointed to be princes. The land was distributed among them so that each one ruled over a large territory.

The most valuable part was their mother's hilltop dwelling place and the land around it. This was granted to Atlas, who as eldest son was the first king. Both the island of Atlantis and the mighty Atlantic Ocean took their names from him. Atlas himself had many sons. Succession to the throne always passed from eldest son to the eldest of his sons.

For generations Atlantis was a peaceful and prosperous kingdom. The yield of its mines and forests, its pasturelands and streams was wonderfully abundant. Wild animals were plentiful. Herds of elephants roamed freely in the deep forests. The food supply was ample for men and all animals, whether wild or domesticated. Anything not provided by the fruitful earth was imported. As Atlantis grew in wealth and influence, its rule extended to many other islands until it reached as far as Italy and Egypt.

When each king ascended to the throne, he made the best possible use of the land and everything it produced. The whole country was organized and beautified according to a careful plan.

First, the kings had bridges built, spanning the rings of water and forming a road leading to and away from the central island. Next they built the royal palace on the inner island.

It stood on the acropolis near the original home of Poseidon and Cleito. Every king received this holy sanctuary as part of his inheritance. He took affectionate pride in trying to surpass whatever his predecessor had done, until in size and in the splendor of their design, the build-

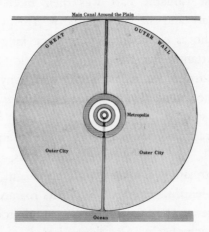

Metropolis, outer city and canal to the sea. (Illustration by Jill Mellick)

ings of the acropolis became a marvel to men's eyes.

Later the kings had a canal dug from the sea to the outermost ring of water. This canal was three hundred feet wide, a hundred feet deep, and fifty stades long. A *stade* is approximately six hundred feet. The canal made the outermost water ring accessible as a harbor to ships at sea. At the bridges, they bored a channel leading from circle to circle which was large enough to allow a trireme to pass through. The channel was roofed over and became an underground tunnel for ships. The rims of the land rings were considerably above sea level.

The largest water ring was three stades wide and the circle of land it enclosed was of equal size. The second water ring measured two stades in width. Again, the land it enclosed was the same width. The water ring surrounding the central island where the palace stood was one stade wide. The island itself had a diameter of five stades.

A wall of stone was built to surround the inner island, its rings, and bridge. Each bridge was fortified with gates and towers at either end. The stone, black, white, and red in color, was quarried beneath the central island as well as the inner and outer land rings. By this process the builders actually excavated two interior basins and roofed them with native rock. The outermost water ring and the middle ring of water thus became docks for ships.

The Atlantean builders enjoyed blending the colorful stones and created patterns in many buildings by combining the colors ornamentally. Sometimes, as if for the sheer fun of it, they would put up a building of one pure color to stand in pleasing contrast to the others.

Finally, a great outer wall was constructed, completely enclosing the Metropolis and outer city of Atlantis.

The Metropolis consisted of the central island and its land and water rings. The outer city of Atlantis was the area between the largest ring and a great outer wall. This huge wall began at the sea. It made a complete circuit at a uniform distance of fifty stades from the outermost ring. Its ends met at the mouth of the canal to the sea. A brass-coated wall encircled the ring where barracks for soldiers and a racecourse were located. Another wall surrounded the inner land ring and was faced with tin. The stone wall protecting the central island had a veneer of orichalcum, the metal known as "mountain bronze," which gave off a soft glow like firelight when the sun's rays caught it. In value orichalcum was second only to gold.

The outer city was densely populated. Ships came and

PLAN OF METROPOLIS
AND OUTER CITY OF ATLANTIS KEY

1. Royal Palace
2. Cleito's Shrine
3. Temple of Poseidon
4. Hot and Cold Springs
5. Gymnasia
6. Gardens
7. Guard Houses

8. Racing Track
9. Tunnels for Ships
10. Walls
11. Fortified Bridges
12. Docks
13. Canal (full length of canal not shown)

A. CENTRAL ISLAND AND ACROPOLIS
B. INNER RING OF WATER
C. MIDDLE RING OF LAND
D. MIDDLE RING OF WATER
E. OUTER RING OF LAND
F. OUTER RING OF WATER
G. OUTER CITY

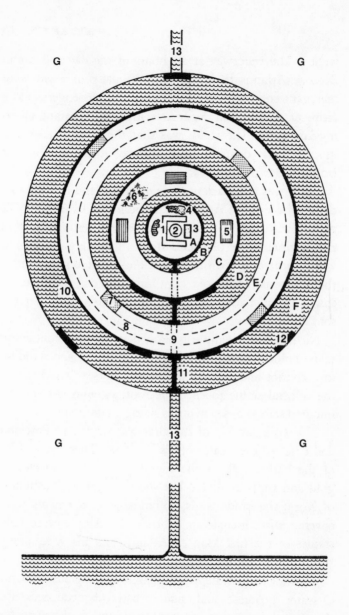

The Metropolis of Atlantis as Plato describes it. (Illustration by Jill Mellick)

went in the waterway at all hours of the day and night. Because Atlantis traded so widely, many of them were merchant ships with foreign crews and passengers. Their frequent arrivals and departures involved constant shouting and noise. The result was that the large harbor and its mercantile quarters were a scene of cheerful uproar from one dawn to the next.

But it was the gracious little central island that became the crown jewel of Atlantis. The buildings of its acropolis glinted with gold. The royal palace was designed so that the original home of Cleito stood in its very center and was dedicated as a shrine to her and Poseidon. Around it the kings placed a golden railing. No one might enter this holy sanctuary, the place where Cleito bore her ten sons.

Nearby was a temple to Poseidon himself, containing many golden statues. The largest was of the god standing in a chariot and driving six winged horses. The head of the colossal statue touched the roof. Around it were one hundred statues of sea nymphs riding on dolphins.

The workmanship of the altar was worthy of Poseidon and reflected the wealth of his kingdom. There was a hint of the barbaric about the temple, with its pinnacles of gold and walls of silver. The interior roof was fashioned of ivory; the inside walls, columns, and pavements were covered with orichalcum. Outside the temple were gold statues of the first king of Atlantis and his wife, along with his princely brothers and their wives.

The hot and cold springs poured out copious amounts of water for indoor and open-air baths. Aqueducts carried the crystal-clear water everywhere. Some baths were for the kings' use only, while others were for private citizens, in addition to some for women. All were set among groves of beautiful trees. There were *gymnasia* and exercise-grounds for men and for horses on each of the land rings, as was suitable for a kingdom established by Poseidon. Since he was the god of horsemanship, he looked with favor on the breeding and training of good steeds. A race-course made a full circuit of the outer ring of land, and on either side of it were barracks for the king's bodyguard. The most trusted of the guards, a picked group of elite men, had their quarters in the royal palace close to the person of the king himself.

From every aspect the Metropolis of Atlantis was bright with flowers and groves of stately trees. Marble temples to many gods had honored places near sparkling pools of water. There was no city to rival the symmetry of its plan and its handsome buildings.

III

The Story Ends Without Ending

The whole region rose high above the sea. Its coast was extremely steep." Plato's account goes on to say that the land about the Metropolis and the outer city was smooth and level. Naturally oblong in shape, this great plain was enclosed on three sides by mountains that went right down to the sea.

The plain was indeed large: in width it measured two hundred and thirty miles. For its full length of three hundred and forty-five miles it faced south, and that sheltered it from the harsh north wind.

The mountains towering above the plain were celebrated for being more numerous, higher, and more beautiful than any that exist today. People living in the mountain villages were unusually prosperous. There were lakes and streams, and the meadows gave good pasturage for their animals. The forests provided timber for every trade and craft.

Thanks to the kings and the plans they carried out for a long period of time, the plain was developed into a rich agricultural area. They trued its oblong shape into a rectangle. A canal was dug on all four sides and the waters of many mountain rivers emptied into it. This canal carried the water southward, toward the city, from both directions. There it was channeled to the sea.

This canal was one hundred feet deep and a good six hundred feet wide. Its length around the four sides of the plain was more than eleven hundred miles.

Channels were cut at regular intervals in the plain, then cross-trenches were added. All told, the canal was intersected by nineteen trenches that went from east to west and twenty-nine from north to south. Timber was floated down from the mountains on these artificial waterways. Boats used them to transport the crops grown on the plain to the city. There was a yield of two harvests yearly. In winter the normal rainfall was dependable; in summer the huge irrigation system assured the farmers of fresh water in whatever amounts they needed.

Plato explains that Atlantis was divided into ten districts. The great plain was one district and was made up of sixty thousand allotments of land. A leader was in charge of each allotment. His duty was to furnish the royal army with fighting men and war equipment.

The supply of men was virtually unlimited in the plain. A man was assigned to his allotment by his own village and district. The allotment leader was obliged to fill a

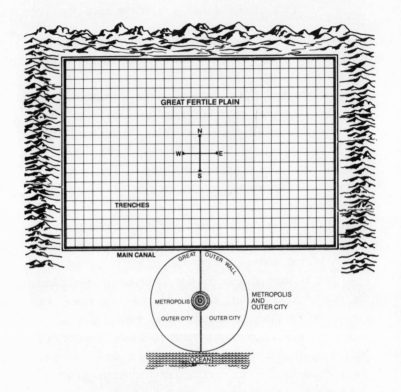

Great fertile plain according to Plato's description. (Illustration by Jill Mellick)

quota of light and heavy war chariots, charioteers, horses and riders, and armed infantrymen called hoplites, who were trained to fight with the sword. The leader also had to supply archers, slingers, and javelin men, as well as marines for the ships of Atlantis. This, according to Plato, is how military arrangements were handled in the plain. He mentions that it had its own Royal City and that arrangements in the other nine districts varied in some respects.

The laws set down by Poseidon called for the rulers of Atlantis to hold regular meetings. The government of the empire was always in the hands of ten men, because in the beginning there were nine princes and the reigning king. They held absolute power of life and death over their subjects. At the appointed times when they met, it was in the temple of Poseidon, where the first kings had inscribed the laws on a pillar of orichalcum. Here they conferred on matters of mutual concern and deliberated on any wrong that one of them might be charged with committing.

Their meetings began with an exchange of pledges as an ancient ceremony required, and it was done in the following way. In the sanctuary of the god a number of consecrated bulls roamed at large. After praying to Poseidon that they might offer a sacrifice that pleased him, the ten rulers started a hunt, using only clubs and nooses because weapons of metal were forbidden.

Once a bull was caught, he was led to the pillar and slaughtered. His throat was slit so that the blood would spill over the pillar of orichalcum and cover the inscription.

The ceremony continued as they made an offering to the god by burning the animal's body. Then a bowl of wine was mixed, and they cast into it a clot of blood for each man present before cleansing the pillar to purify it. The rest of the blood was consumed by the flames while the wine was served in golden cups. A libation was poured over the fire, and each ruler took his oath to give judgment according to the laws written on the pillar. They vowed to punish anyone who had been disobedient to the laws and promised that they themselves would not wilfully disobey them. Their final pledge was they would never give or obey any command that violated the laws of their father Poseidon. When each man completed his vows he drank the wine and dedicated his cup as a gift to the temple.

After dining together, and when the sacrificial fire was beginning to die down, they put on magnificent blue robes. They seated themselves on the ground by the glowing embers to wait until the temple grew dark. Then they were ready to hear any charges of law-breaking or complaints made against them. Later, in the light of the new day, they wrote their decisions on a gold tablet. This and their robes they dedicated to Poseidon as a record of their work.

Among the laws that defined their authority, the most important were these: they would not make war on each other but would come to one another's defense if someone tried to overthrow the ruler of any district. But if that should happen, they were to follow the custom of their ancestors and confer together, clearly recognizing that the chief command belonged to the house of Atlas. The king of that house, however, had no authority to put to death any of his royal brothers unless a majority of the others gave their consent.

This is the way power was balanced and held in that part of the world. It was the full weight of this tremendous power that went into the sudden attack on the Athenians.

Just as long as they kept alive the noble spark of divinity they inherited from Poseidon, the kings of Atlantis were faithful to his laws and honored him. They treated one another considerately and wisely. They ruled well. The changes fortune might bring they could bear with dignity, because they believed that what counted above all else were certain qualities of character. Their integrity meant more than riches or power. While these ideals guided their lives, the Atlantean rulers lived at peace among themselves and dealt fairly with all other people.

But that spark of the divine nature within them began to flicker and grow dim because of their marriages with mortals. Finally it died out. Then it was that they behaved not at all like the god who was their forefather, but like ordinary foolish humans. They forgot their pledges and ceased to be a people of moderation. At the very moment in their history when they appeared to be blessed with happiness and prosperity, the rulers of Atlantis were actually tainted with pride. Ambition overcame restraint, and they reached out for even greater power.

This change in them was beheld by Zeus, the god of gods. What they had become, after turning from the commandments of their ancestors, was highly displeasing to him. He saw them as men in an evil condition. They must be curbed and disciplined, made to return to the laws they had recklessly abandoned.

Zeus was about to pronounce punishment on Atlantis. He had assembled all the Olympian gods around him at his royal residence, which stands at the center of the universe, and they were waiting to hear his judgment.

Plato's story concludes with these words:

". . . *and when he* (Zeus) *had gathered them to-gether, he said* . . ."

And there Plato's history of Atlantis ends. Or rather, it does not end. It stops.

IV

The Birth of the Legend

The abrupt way this account is cut short leaves any reader surprised and puzzled. Did Plato do it deliberately, to heighten the drama of that last scene? Had he intended to finish the story later but for some reason did not return to it? The reply to both questions has to be "Nobody knows."

Whether Atlantis was wholly imagined by Plato or based by him on facts known at that time, he had made the island-continent immortal by writing about it. To those who willingly believed in it, Atlantis was a real place, although every trace of it had vanished. Time after time the will to believe in an actual Atlantis has been a stronger influence than the best efforts of skeptics to dismiss it as a charming fantasy.

One reason this belief has lasted out the centuries is that

Plato told his tale so persuasively. First of all he was generous, even lavish, with details. Not content just to describe buildings and natural or man-made landmarks, he more often than not gives their precise measurements. He is quite specific about the design and dimensions of the Metropolis and the great fertile plain. Plato was a poet, and he permits his readers tantalizing glimpses of landscapes that have a dreamlike quality about them. They are not altogether familiar but they are not quite unfamiliar, either.

For example, when he writes of the fertile plain that produced two crops yearly, he calls it a rectangular area 2,000 by 3,000 stades in size. As a unit of measurement the stade is about 606 Greek feet, and the Greek foot differs from the American by about an inch. In round numbers ten stades are approximately one mile.

If anybody takes the simple step of converting a few of these measurements into actual miles, he is due for a surprise. A land area of 2,000 by 3,000 stades would be 230 by 345 statute miles, or 79,350 square miles. That would be a piece of real estate 2,000 square miles *larger* than Nebraska, and it could readily include Rhode Island as well! Figures like these conjure up a farming region vastly larger than any that could have been under cultivation on the mainland of Greece at that time or any of its islands.

Plato brings the picture of this land into sharp focus: ". . . *The region was protected from the cold north winds.*" It rose steeply from the sea and stood high above it; even so, the great plain was surrounded by soaring mountains on all sides but the south. Because these mountains were ". . . *more numerous, higher, and more beau-*

tiful than any that exist today," they were much admired by visitors from distant lands.

This exactness of detail has convinced the believers that Plato was describing a major island or continent, and the measurements "prove" it. Doubters reply that Plato didn't worry his head about measurements because the story was made up; from start to finish, it was all imaginary, and that "proves" *their* point. Nothing at all is proved by such arguments—except that people like to argue. Evidence is not proof, and in this and other instances, the distinction should be kept in mind.

The more closely one looks at the original story, the more there is to question. The military organization of Atlantis sounds almost Spartan, but Sparta, or for that matter Athens, did not exist at the time in which Plato set Atlantis, 9000 B.C.

One question leads to another. How could it be that the Atlanteans were master craftsmen and builders when elsewhere in the world of 9,000 B.C. men were struggling to cut wood with stone axes and hunt game with primitive bows and arrows? Who could have taught architectural planning to the Atlanteans of the New Stone Age period? Where did they acquire their technical knowhow in engineering, agriculture, and irrigation? From whom could they learn about shipbuilding and navigation? Had they made all these discoveries by themselves, only to have them perish along with their civilization in the course of one day and one night?

When the land trembled and sank, might there have been a few lucky survivors? What became of them? Are the fragments of their stone buildings lying on some ocean floor?

Captain Nemo, who is the hero of Jules Verne's novel, *Twenty Thousand Leagues Under the Sea,* takes a friend on an underwater diving expedition in Chapter 9, Part II of that book. A moving and eerie scene follows when the captain guides him to a sunken city—"a perfect Pompeii" —whose location is known only to the master of the submarine *Nautilus.* He has found Atlantis. Among its ruins an undersea volcano spews forth torrents of lava. The submerged city is part of a lost continent that once lay, as Plato said, beyond the Pillars of Hercules.

Fanciful scenes of this sort in novels and stories have kept the legend active and added immeasureably to its glamour. It has as surely shaped men's dreams as it has been shaped by them.

Although Plato's account is barely fifty pages long, the legend that grew around it has never been successfully explained or laughed out of existence.

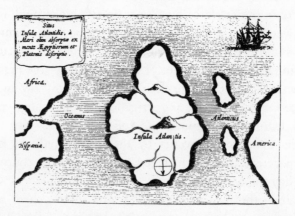

An early map of Atlantis, made in 1665. Note that compass directions are reversed: North is South. (Courtesy of Mansell Collection)

V

The Legend Grows Tall

"*It is possible that the story . . . of Atlantis is not fiction.*" So wrote a scientist of the second century B.C. He had been the tutor of the young Roman orator, Cicero, and his name was Poseidonius. (No relation to Poseidon so far as anyone knows!) The earth sciences were his specialty. This view of his, expressed in one of his many books, gave another boost to the increasingly popular idea that Plato had reported history.

The Greek geographer and historian Strabo was a contemporary of Jesus. He believed that Plato had based his story on solid historical rock. Few denials came from writers and scientists during the time Rome ruled the Mediterranean world. Plutarch, the Greek biographer, put into words what many have felt after reading Plato's account. He spoke of the sense of regret one has that it is not finished, ". . . because the satisfaction he [Plato] takes in what is complete is extraordinary."

Pliny the Elder was a Roman historian who had a few doubts about Atlantis, but he didn't deny that it could have existed. "The island did indeed sink," he wrote, "if we are to believe Plato." In 79 A.D. Pliny went to the Bay of Naples by ship so that he could be an eye-witness to the eruption of Mount Vesuvius that buried Pompeii and Herculaneum. His scientific curiosity cost him his life. Along with many others, he was trapped near the Bay when its waters became stormy and the air so dense with poisonous fumes that no ship could come ashore to rescue him. He was one of the volcano's countless victims.

In the scientific circles of Greece and Rome, those who accepted Plato's Atlantis story as factual outnumbered the doubters. Roman historians gradually swung around to treat everything that Plato wrote as though it had been divinely inspired. He became fashionable and infallible, an authority not to be questioned. What a fate for a philosopher like Plato—to become a fad!

An Alexandrian monk of the sixth century, Cosmas by name, declared that the Atlantis tale proved the accuracy of the Bible. To his way of thinking, Plato had his facts correct but his sources muddled. Cosmas was sure that the floods Plato mentioned were those that put Noah to sea in the Ark. Over the centuries, the Atlantis legend would be used to support many quaint theories, but Cosmas was the first to relate it to the Bible.

After the collapse of Rome's farflung empire, the Atlantis legend went into temporary eclipse. The Christian Church encouraged people to put aside their concern with things of this world and concentrate on what was to come in the life after death. Heaven and hell were matters more urgent than stories of a lost island.

Still, European traders carried their wares to foreign countries and commerce slowly expanded. The Crusades inspired a sudden upswing in travel. Soldiers and pilgrims by the thousands were on the move to foreign lands. The old rumors about Atlantis were revived while men journeyed far from their homelands and rubbed elbows with people whose customs were alien to their own. Religious pilgrimages took people away from their isolated hamlets. It was an expanding, changing world, and the changes had profound effects on men's lives.

After the voyages of Columbus the Atlantis legend came back to life with a burst of energy. Mariners were undertaking longer and more risky voyages, now that they knew they could return safely home without falling off the edge of a flat earth. The Sargasso Sea in the North Atlantic filled sailors with the fear that their vessels might get hopelessly caught in the tentacles of floating seaweed. But nobody slid off the rim of the world, and no one could verify reports of any ships being swallowed either by seaweed or monsters.

Among the navigational charts used by Columbus was one drawn in 1475. It showed groups of islands dotting the Atlantic to the west of Europe. One island, Antilia, was thought by many sailors to be Atlantis. Rumor had it shimmering with gold and said that its name came from the word *Atlantis*. It still can be found on modern maps as the Antilles, or West Indies.

If any one man deliberately set out to hunt for Atlantis in those years, there is no record. But the legend was more alluring than ever, for Columbus had proved the world to be larger, more complex, and peopled with creatures more various than anyone had imagined. Eddies of excitement swept through the oldest cities of Europe whenever ships returned from lengthy voyages.

Crewman bragged of seeing incredible sights. Sailors are notorious as tale-tellers. The seas, they said, were infested with monsters. Unknown lands sighted from their ships' rails were inhabited by beings dressed in animal skins and smeared with paint. They had seen cannibals and heard the sounds of creatures more like beasts than humans, who communicated in grunts and snorts. Some were one-eyed, said the sailors, while some had only one leg and were horrible to behold. Map makers turned out maps that were influenced by the stories of mariners who had seen fantastic things and lived to tell of them.

The wrangle over the shape of the earth—round, disk-shaped, or flat—was drawing to an end with the voyages of discovery. Columbus himself thought that the earth was pear-shaped. He was convinced that his ships traveled uphill when he sailed *west* and on the return voyage, sailing *east,* he was coasting downhill to Spain. He believed that the original Garden of Eden was to be found in the land where the mighty Orinoco River rises, which we know as Venezuela. He had seen that river's mouth and thought it part of an unexplored continent. Man's original earthly Paradise, he believed, lay in the interior of that land from which its waters poured.

In 1553, a Spaniard named Francesco Lopez de Gómara wrote in a history of the Indies that the New World was actually Atlantis. Gómara had served for a time as Cortés's personal secretary and wrote an account of his life. That a man of his prominence held this view is significant; the

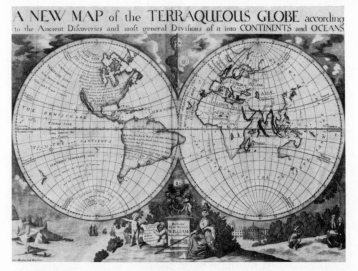

A world map made in England, 1718. It shows the globe "according to the ancient discoveries," when the North American continent was generally unknown. The map-maker adds his own opinion that there are some who think the entire continent was the ancient island of Atlantis.
(Courtesy of Mr. and Mrs. M. H. L. Sanders, Jr.)

Atlantis legend had plowed steadily along in the wake of west-bound ships.

As the map on this page shows, even by 1718 so little was understood about the actual size and shape of North America that a British map maker printed these words across the entire northwest segment:

> *"This Continent with the adjoining Islands is generally supposed to have been Anciently unknown*

*though there are not wanting some, who will have
even the Continent its self to be no other than the
Insula ATLANTIS of the Ancients."*

It is amusing to note that the map's designer was not
saying "This *is* Atlantis," but neither was he ruling out
that wonderful possibility.

Plato's tale has inspired so many hundreds of books
and stories that their exact number is beyond reckoning.
By the 1950s there were more than two thousand. Among
these, two are centuries-old classics that reveal how popular the Atlantis legend was during the Renaissance.
Utopia, by Sir Thomas More, appeared first in Latin in the
year 1516, then had many translations. Its title means
"No Place," combining as it does the Greek word for no
(*ou*) with *topos,* meaning place. The story is about an
imaginary island where men strive to make their government and laws as perfect as they can. Poverty and injustice
are unknown. Utopia's good life is contrasted with social
conditions in the England of More's day.

The year 1624 saw the publication of Sir Francis Bacon's *The New Atlantis,* a tale of the adventures that be-
fall fifty-one Europeans sailing from Peru to China. When
their ship is blown off course, they land in a country called
Bensalem. The castaways are welcomed by a group of
devout Christians, descendants of the original Atlanteans.
They inform their guests that Atlantis used to be in the
region of the Americas now covered by Peru and Mexico.
A flood had driven out their forefathers. (Any version of
the Atlantis story without a flood in it somewhere is a
novelty!) Under the leadership of one saintly man they
founded New Atlantis, and they want no contact with
people of other nations. In their knowledge of science

and in spiritual understanding they are light-miles ahead of the rest of humanity.

The European visitors are treated to unusual sights in one of Bensalem's cities. Miraculous cures are available for any illness. A "Water of Paradise" prolongs life. Furnaces produce precious gems and rare metals. The people of New Atlantis have mastered the secrets of flying like birds and swimming like fish of the deep.

"We also have means to convey sounds in trunks and pipes, in strange lines and distances" a leader explains to the guests. Some buildings reach a half mile into the sky. Beneath them are refrigerated caves where bodies are conserved. With their daring scientific experiments the New Atlanteans are patiently unlocking one after another of nature's secrets.

The Europeans wander through art galleries containing statues of renowned inventors. Bensalem's citizens are informed about everything that has gone on in the outside world. "There we have the statue of your Columbus . . . your Monk that was the inventor of ordnance and gunpowder . . . the inventor of printing . . . the inventor of silk of the worm . . ." This early science-fiction tale ends with the words, "The rest was not perfected," another way of saying that it is unfinished—like Plato's own story.

Bacon was one of the first writers to endow his Atlanteans with powers akin to magic. Their experiments suggest the work of alchemists, while to modern readers their machines resemble planes, submarines, radio, and radar. Bacon gracefully carried forward the tradition that their knowledge was superhuman, and he made them appealing to men of the Renaissance era. Both *Utopia* and *The New Atlantis* show the far-reaching influence of

Plato. Bacon's little classic gave to the legend that inspired it an extra measure of esteem and acceptance.

And the maps—handsome, decorative, and artistic in design—kept coming from the presses. One printed in France in 1769 showed the Americas to be a single continent neatly parceled into ten segments. These were, naturally, the divisions the god Poseidon had made of his kingdom for his ten sons! This map maker must have spent much of his time with sea-faring men. Scientists who were his contemporaries considered the map a joke, and they said so.

The point is, however, that the Atlantis legend had followed the explorers' ships throughout the years of discovery and exploration. The Atlantic Ocean had been crossed. The next chapters in the career of the legend were written on the American continent.

VI

New Lands and Old Ruins

Columbus died a disappointed man. On none of his four voyages had he found India. He had failed to reach the marvelous Cipango, or Japan, of Marco Polo. The land of silk and jade, called Cathay, had eluded him. But to the day of his death in 1506 he clung to the belief that he had set foot on islands off the coast of Asia, and he had named their inhabitants "Indians."

It took several decades to clear away the uncertainties that troubled Columbus. Before Europeans could gain an understanding of the New World's magnitude, there had to be Balboa's heart-stopping discovery of the Pacific Ocean in 1513. Its very existence had not been suspected. After that came the long, perilous, and tragic voyage of Magellan, who sailed around the most southerly cape of South America while trying to circle the globe. Not until that venture ended, with its commander dead and only a handful of the crew still alive, did navigators realize how wrong their maps and charts were.

The major flaw in them all was that the continents were made to appear much larger than the earth's water areas. This mistake of the ancient geographers was monotonously repeated for centuries. Even when corrections were made, places called *Atlantis* kept bobbing up on the pretty charts. Shown either as a tiny speck of land or a huge territory labeled "unknown" or "unexplored," Atlantis surfaced here and there like a playful dolphin.

Early in the sixteenth century the Spanish made heavy investments of their manpower and energy to explore the more promising regions of the New World. By 1517 the rumors that there was much gold in the Aztec cities of Mexico drew an iron-willed soldier named Hernan Cortés at the head of a small but seasoned army to Tenochtitlán, the Mexican capital. Cortés was a stocky, broad-shouldered man with a deceptively friendly manner. He found the Aztecs a highly advanced people. He left their finest cities captive and their proud leaders dead or in chains.

Among the Aztecs there was an old legend that foretold the coming of strange white gods who would destroy them. Without the Indians' fatalistic belief in that legend, the white invaders' conquest could not have been so overwhelming. Cortés also had help from some native tribes who wanted freedom from Aztec domination and were willing to follow his command.

It is said that on an August day in 1521 the eyes of Cortés were brimming with tears when he murmured that the Aztec city of Tenochtitlán was "one of the most beautiful sights in the world." He wept to see it in flames. But it was he who had just given the order that it be burned to the ground as a sign that henceforth he was the new ruler.

Driven by the same harsh will to conquer, a former Spanish cattle breeder by the name of Francisco Pizarro overcame the Incas. Their empire stretched up and down the coast of Peru for more than two thousand miles. The story of their downfall has the same themes of treachery and deceit that bloody the pages of history as Cortés wrote it in Mexico. However, Pizarro did not burn the Inca capital when he entered it, and he generously allowed the fallen Indian ruler to be strangled instead of burned at the stake.

The Spanish conquistadors brought with them soldier-secretaries who took notes on the astonishing size and beauty of Indian cities. Their reports made mention of the Indian-artisans' work in fabrics, feathers, and gold. Nobody was prepared to behold such cities or gold in such staggering amounts.

Between them, the Spanish and Portuguese hurriedly staked out broad expanses of the New World as their exclusive property. There was gold to be taken, much gold. They looked upon the Indians as heathens who would have to be converted to the white man's religion.

One question arose during the conquest and would be asked again and again when cargoes of gold and jewels reached Europe from the sacked cities of Mexico and Peru. *Who were these Indians?*

The Maya of Yucatán, like the Incas, had networks of roads to connect their towns. Those of the Incas were so good that they rivaled the old Roman highways of Europe. Irrigation systems and aqueducts were in wide use.

In Yucatán the Maya priests jealously guarded collections of their sacred books. These were made of long strips of paper called *huun,* the pounded pulp of fig tree fibers, folded and encased in wooden covers. All Maya books were written—actually they were painted— in pictographic symbols and characters. The books dealt with magic and religious ceremonials, with astronomy and the calendar. Many symbols that appeared in the books were carved into intricate designs on temple walls and stone monuments.

The writing had meaning only to the Indian priests and some of the nobles. Commoners could not read. As for the conquistadors, they showed no interest in books or weirdly beautiful stone carvings. Not with so much golden treasure dazzling them.

But there were others who wondered about the past of the Maya. *Who were these Indians?* They were not ignorant "savages" and there was more than one nation of them. The Incas had little direct contact with the Aztecs. Their languages and modes of life were different. Before the Spanish learned much that was significant about the Maya or the Aztecs and Incas, men thousands of miles across the sea kept asking *Who were they?*

Their weapons were no match for the white conqueror with his horses, his steel armor and gunpowder. Yet the most illiterate Spanish footsoldier could see for himself as he fingered his heavy musket that the dark-skinned men whose towns he was paid to attack were anything but "barbarians." Their elegant temple-cities had not sprung up in the jungles overnight. There was a long history to them, but nobody knew what it was. Chichén Itzá in northern Yucatán was a metropolis of grand design, although the conquistadors found it barren and deserted when they fought a furious battle on the staircase of one of its ruined pyramids. Who had constructed these buildings? Why had they been abandoned?

Who were these Indians?

The secretaries' reports were filed in Spain. They had been prepared for the king. Once read, they went to dusty shelves in dark libraries to lie there forgotten. A few Europeans were privileged to see examples of the Aztecs' work in gold before the sculptured figures of animals and the delicate jewel-encrusted ornaments were hammered down and melted into ingots for the royal treasury. They also examined two of the Aztecs' paper books that were sent as curiosities. These were evidence of a high order of learning, and the workmanship of the art objects was superlative. The Old World craftsmen and scholars readily recognized their value. They, too, wanted to know *Who were these Indians?* The next question was inevitable: *Where had they come from?*

For the white man who "discovered" the advanced Indian cultures, it was natural to look for an origin *outside* the Americas. It was both easy and convenient for them in their arrogant ignorance to decide that these cultures had stemmed from older civilizations of the known world or were transplants of them.

This was a time when educated European gentlemen were well acquainted with the literature of the Bible. The works of classical Greek and Roman writers were being read again after centuries of neglect. They turned to these sources in trying to account for the native civilizations that they were at a loss to explain.

In this manner myth and legend get hopelessly tangled

with historical fact. Events in the Americas were moving faster than men had the means to record them or the ability to interpret them with insight. There were also, of course, ancient Asian and African civilizations about which they had only hazy ideas, no clear or reliable information. For these reasons and others, the *Who were they?* question turned into a scholarly guessing game with religious and racial overtones.

One of the first persons to wrestle seriously with the problem of who the Indians were and where they had come from was Bishop Diego de Landa, a Spanish missionary of the Franciscan order. He lived many years among the Maya people without being able to find an answer to either question, though he gave each of them much thought. This devout man could not guess that centuries later his nearly forgotten writings would be used to bolster the claim that the Maya had come from Plato's lost Atlantis. Inadvertently, the Bishop had granted the Atlantis legend a permanent lease on life in the New World. And all the while his mind was on the saving of souls, not on rumors and superstitions about an ancient island.

VII

Lost Books and Lost Tribes

The young missionary friar who went to Yucatán in 1550 had one consuming purpose. His sole aim was to convert the "heathen" to Christianity. Diego de Landa was determined to win the Maya away from their worship of idols and put a stop to human sacrifice, the gruesome practice they carried out to appease their gods.

He was a dedicated man. In twelve years he rose from one position of authority to another, and by 1562 he was the Bishop of Yucatán. As he lived and worked among the Maya, Landa came to think that there was a long and turbulent history behind them, although not even the oldest of the old people knew anything beyond legends and folktales about it. Each phase of their life had its fixed ritual or ceremony. The Maya priests saw to their strict observance.

Bishop Landa could sense that Maya civilization had passed its peak and was declining. He was intuitively right. Historians now think that it had reached a "golden age" in the ninth century A.D. Everything this acutely observant man saw convinced him that the sacred painted books of the priests, valued by them above gold, held clues to that unknown past. The Maya possessed so little gold anyway that it did not tempt the conquistadors. No jeweled treasures of theirs were shipped to Spain to fill the king's coffers.

The Bishop grew increasingly uneasy about the native priests and their influence, but even more ill at ease about their painted books. It was as though these objects of wood and paper had some diabolical power to stand like a wall of stone between him and the conversion of all the Maya. He learned with horror that some Indians were still worshiping their gods in well-hidden temples. Worse yet, in spite of his best efforts, human victims were being slain.

When Bishop Landa found a large collection of priestly books in one Maya town, he gave an order that reveals the depth of his frustration and his fanatical intensity. The books must be burned. All of them. Later he wrote, ". . . they contained nothing in which there were not to be seen superstition and lies of the devil." And burned they were, heaped into a huge blazing pyre in the town plaza.

The Maya's response caught him by surprise. He wrote that this was an action ". . . they regretted to an amazing degree, and which caused them much affliction." Also it brought wrathful criticism from some of his religious brethren, who said that he was overstepping his authority. At length this very charge was made by high Church officials in Spain. Landa went there to conduct his own defense, won his case, then returned to resume his labors in Yucatán.

No one person left such extensive reporting on the Maya of the sixteenth century as Bishop Landa. Neither did any one man do more to wipe out their written literature. Only three complete books dating from pre-conquest days are known to have escaped his torch. They are estimated to be at least seven hundred years old.

This man of many contradictions finally turned to the serious study of Maya folkways and traditions. Whether it was the Indians' distress or the disapproval of his peers

PAGES OF MAYA PROPHECY FROM THE DRESDEN CODEX

A FARMER'S ALMANAC PAGE. *Torches held by a dog and a parrot (center) are fire signs. This page of water and fire signs was used by Maya priests to forecast weather conditions for farmers.* (All photographs pages 45-48 courtesy of Sächsische Landesbibliothek, Dresden, German Democratic Republic.)

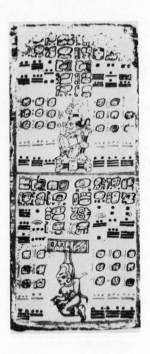

A PAGE OF LUNAR ECLIPSES. *Eclipses of the moon were thought to cause terrible disasters. The dates of lunar eclipses are foretold on this page by dot and bar symbols, which are numerals. The death god sits on a chair of human bones.*

A PROPHECY OF WAR. *From top to bottom, note the warrior attacked by spear-throwers; the dying deer; a god seated on a throne made of a serpent, and a bound captive. This page warns of future wars and droughts.*

RABBIT AND SERPENT PAGE.
The rain god and rabbit wear headdresses used in New Year ceremonies. Pairs of numbers near the serpents refer to a date thousands of years in the past and important in the Maya calendar. The page is a series of mathematical calculations.

A PREDICTION OF ANNUAL RAINS. *Flood waters spill on the earth from the mouth of a dragon. A goddess which claws for feet pours water from a jar. This page, with its reminder of the great flood that the Maya thought destroyed the earth, was used to predict the date of the annual rainy season.*

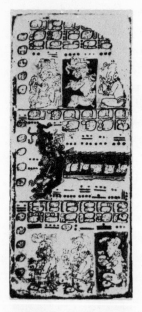 

A PROPHECY OF LUCKY AND UNLUCKY DAYS. *Two pages used by Maya priests to give the dates of lucky and unlucky days. Various gods are represented. Dot and bar symbols are numbers indicating the calendar day for each prophecy.*

---

that moved him, Bishop Landa began compiling records about Maya life as diligently as he had worked to counteract the influence of their books. Historians praise him for the one activity but they have regretful and sometimes harsh words for the other.

When he put his mind to the task of learning Maya writing, Landa tried to devise an alphabet that he hoped would be the key for translating it into Spanish. He was keenly aware that the books were revered by their priests because they dealt with ". . . ancient affairs and their sciences." As he said, ". . . with these and drawings and with certain signs in these drawings, they understood their affairs and made others understand them and taught them."

The surviving books are for the most part religious and astronomical. They are based on the calculations of their astronomers, who were amazingly skillful observers. They divided time into periods of twenty years, called *katuns*. A year consisted of 360 days. The Mayas thought that all history repeated itself; events occurring in one future *katun* would repeat all the events of another in the ancient past. Their fascination with the past grew out of this belief, and their priests claimed to have the gift of prophesying the future.

Maya astronomers could predict eclipses of the sun, the moon, and many planets with startling accuracy. To the native priests, the brightly painted books were essential as their guides in performing their religious duties. If there were other kinds of records, and there probably were, they have vanished. The photographs on pages 45–48 are pages from one of the "books of prophecy." It dates from the thirteenth century.

Bishop Landa had often watched the Maya priests as they unfolded their books, burning incense and chanting prayers before they read aloud their forecast of what was to come. Afterward they would suggest to their people various ways to ward off the dangers and evils foretold in the painted pages.

By seizing so many of the books the Bishop had undermined the power of the priests; no question about that. Now he was bent on discovering what the Maya alphabet was. Once he found that, he believed that he would have the key for translating Maya into Spanish. Far more urgently for his purpose, he could then translate Spanish into the Maya written language. Nothing would speed him more swiftly to his goal of winning converts.

In assuming that the strange writing had an alphabet, as ours does, he made a costly mistake. Not all forms of writing, particularly the oldest, use an alphabet. Maya writing is one of these.

It was hieroglyphic. Pictures were used for words. The word for *road,* for example is simply the picture of a road. But the writing also used phonetics; different signs represented different sounds. Sometimes the Maya used both—hieroglyphic and phonetic. In this way they could express abstract ideas whose meanings could not be shown by pictures alone.

The Bishop never understood how complicated the system was. Although he thought he had worked out an alphabet, he had not. But he did make hundreds of hand-drawn copies of the symbols and characters. Just as carefully he noted those that stood for numerals, for days and months. In a book entitled *Relación de las Cosas de Yucatán*—Account of the Things of Yucatán—he included his alphabet "key" to the language, faulty and fragmentary though it was. The section of his book that created a stir when other churchmen read it was this one:

"Some of the old people say that they have heard from their ancestors that this land was occupied by a race of people who came from the East and whom God had delivered by opening twelve paths through

the sea. If this were true, it necessarily follows that
all the inhabitants of the Indes [sic] *are descendants*
of the Jews . . ."

Bishop Landa's words were pounced on by others who
saw in them a way to link Indian Americans with an ancient Old World civilization. Never mind his cautious,
qualifying words, *"If this were true,"* because nobody
noticed them then or later! The idea became a theory. It
supplied an instant answer to the two pesky questions:
Who were these Indians? and *Where had they come from?*

The Jews mentioned by the Bishop were a group of
people, 27,290 all told, who were torn away from Sa-
maria, a city in the Northern Kingdom of Israel, in the
year 721 B.C. Their story is told in two books of the Old
Testament: Kings II and Chronicles I. The captured
Israelites came to be called the Lost Ten Tribes of Israel.
What happened to them has been debated so long that it
is one of history's most elderly question marks.

Historians cannot take the Lost Tribes theory seriously
to account for the origin of any Indian Americans. They
explain the disappearance of the tribes by pointing out
that, when the captives and their descendants intermar-
ried, they adopted the customs of the regions that are now
Iraq and Iran. They could not have carried on their own
cultural heritage in alien lands. Another reason they were
called "lost" is far simpler: they had strayed from their
religion. To do him justice, the Bishop was offering nothing more than an offhand comment as he conscientiously
wrote down what he had been told. Elsewhere in his *Re-*

lación he stated firmly that the builders of the great Maya structures were Indians.

Another theory, less popular than the one attributed to the Bishop, claimed that the Indians weren't Jews, but Assyrians. Wasn't the facial structure of the Maya like that of the Assyrians?

The *Who were they?* game appealed then, as it still does, to people with a fondness for romantic solutions to knotty historical problems. Various "experts" have argued that the Americas were populated by descendants of the Trojans, the Norsemen, or the Japanese. One Spanish friar who also was concerned with the matter of origins wrote in 1607 that some Indians ". . . have probably descended from the Carthaginians, others from the lost Atlantis, from the Greeks, from the Phoenicians and still others from the Chinese, Tartars, and other groups." It would be a long while before anyone made a case for Atlantis as the Maya's homeland. When it happened, the idea sprang directly from the Bishop's writings.

By an odd quirk of history, it was Bishop Landa's alphabet "key" that swept the Atlantis legend into the broad stream of theories about Indian origins. By an even odder quirk, the Bishop's own writings, lost soon after his death, stayed lost for three hundred years. They were found by another man of the Church, Charles Étienne Brasseur. The painstaking study Brasseur made of the "key" alphabet prompted him to make a solemn announcement. The Maya were neither Israelites nor Egyptians, as had also been claimed. Their true ancestors, he said, were more remote and more glamorous than the Israelites: they had come to Yucatán from Atlantis.

This was easily the most thrilling theory of them all to

those who longed for a neat, tidy, and romantic answer. One magic word—*Atlantis*—answered the *Who were they?* and *Where had they come from?* questions. The flickering spark of hope that there had been survivors of the Atlantis disaster flared up brightly.

VIII

New Lives for an Old Legend

The belief that he has found the missing key or the hidden clue to a mystery can lead the unwary seeker down a false trail. Anyone following such a trail may become unwilling to abandon it even if he suspects it is the wrong one.

This all too human tendency did not escape the notice of the shrewd American showman, P. T. Barnum. In the 1850s he displayed a pair of "royal Aztec children" in his New York museum. His flashy advertisements claimed that they had been "kidnapped from hostile Indians" in the Mexican jungles, where they were found in "a living Aztec city" filled with "statues of the ancient kings of Assyria." Hundreds of cash customers lined up to marvel and stare at the children. Barnum knew how to dupe people and make them enjoy it. He liked to say, "There's a sucker born every minute."

Some men make money and fame by deceiving others. Some create tragedy by deceiving themselves. The Atlantis legend has been a magnet for both kinds.

In 1865, Charles Étienne Brasseur discovered Bishop Landa's book about the Mayas. It had lain unnoticed for better than three hundred years in the library of Madrid's Historical Academy. A respected historian and an abbé, or official, of the French church, Brasseur thought that he had found a priceless document. His excitement was not dulled when the book proved to be a shortened version of the lost *Relaçion de las Cosas de Yucatán,* because it contained the Bishop's "key" to Maya writing. This was a rare prize.

Brasseur dared to believe that with the key he could read the old Maya books. The very disappearance of Bishop Landa's book gave it special and unmerited importance. Scientists of many disciplines accorded his alphabet a value out of all proportion to its worth. They were delighted at Brasseur's wonderful luck.

The Abbé secluded himself to begin his absorbing task of working with the surviving Maya books. First he published Landa's "key." Then he started to publish the translations he made with its help, page after page of what he said were Maya myths and creation legends.

His friends were deeply troubled. The translations were nothing more than rambling nonsense. What had happened to this brilliant scholar? Others tried to work with the Landa alphabet and said flatly that it was useless. They dismissed it and Brasseur's work as a waste of time.

His life for the next decade was one of strained and lonely isolation, but he went on with the translations. Out of respect for his past achievements, his critics kept silent.

He didn't understand. He was hurt. In one Maya text he found a pair of hieroglyphs that "spelled" the word *Mu*. It was, he said, the name of a land utterly destroyed by floods. He saw many similarities between the land of Mu and Atlantis and wrote glowingly about them. His friends were even more saddened. He was a changed man, bent on doing a hopeless and useless task. At last Brasseur's own doubts began to undermine his belief in the worth of all he had studied and written.

In this crisis he turned to mysticism. He managed to convince himself that the translations revealed that Mu was really Atlantis, and it was the source of America's native Indian cultures. He wrote of an "Atlantean race" that survived a prehistoric flood in the New World. A few escaped death and sailed to Africa, where they founded the civilization of Egypt.

He wrote endlessly, on and on. The Maya and Mexican gods, he said, represented natural forces such as hurricanes, volcanoes, and earthquakes. These had destroyed Atlantis. Brasseur slipped further into fantasy. His final verdict was that Mu and not Atlantis was the correct name of the land that floods overwhelmed.

Brasseur deceived himself and became lost in his inner world of doubt and conflict. He died a bitter, confused man who never knew that his final work was met with stony silence because his critics were being compassionate.

Modern language experts are constantly studying the surviving Maya writings. Russian linguists have even put computers to work on the problem. Large segments of the priestly books still defy translation, but progress has been made. That encourages the patient scholars who work with them to predict that someday the books can be read in full.

The land of Mu did not die with Brasseur. One of his fellow countrymen made the Mu theory part and parcel of still another version of the Atlantis legend. This man was Augustus Le Plongeon. He was not by nature gentle, like Brasseur, and he was as arrogant as Brasseur was shy. He always signed himself "Doctor," tacking an LL.D. after his signature to serve notice that he was also a lawyer. Nobody knew where or whether he had earned those degrees.

Le Plongeon managed to wrap both Atlantis and Mu into one bulky package while he rewrote history according to his own whims. He insisted that refugees from both Atlantis and Mu had founded the Maya civilization. Later, their colonists went from Yucatán to settle in Africa, where they inspired Egypt's imposing culture. If the theme is familiar, it is because Le Plongeon borrowed so heavily from those last sorry writings of Brasseur.

His schooling was in military science and mathematics. Far from being a hobby, the study of Mexican antiquities was Le Plongeon's ruling passion. From 1875 on, he and his American wife spent more than thirty years exploring Maya ruins. He married her when she was seventeen and he forty-seven. Alice Le Plongeon believed with all her heart that he was discovering momentous historical truths. As a mystic she accepted them whole-heartedly.

Many of his ideas came to him while they lived in tents or decaying temples at places like Uxmal and Chichén Itzá. He was a storm-center of controversy. Le Plongeon was never happier than when he was at swords' points with historians or with officials of the Mexican government, who suspected him of plotting to steal some of *their*, not *his*, ancient statues. In those thirty years Le Plongeon concocted a version of world history that blew up a minor tempest when he published it. Another whirled about him with his book called *Queen Moo and the Egyptian Sphinx*. This one featured a Queen Moo, or Mu, who was born a Maya princess of Chichén Itzá. In a story resembling science fiction, it told how Atlantean refugees settled in Yucatán 11,500 years ago. They became the Maya. Princess Moo fled from a civil war, tried vainly to find Atlantis, and at length reached Egypt, where Maya-Egyptian settlers along the banks of the Nile crowned her their Queen and hailed her as "Isis." Le Plongeon explained to his ignorant readers that this meant "Little Sister."

The book included his own drawings of Maya temple designs. These, he argued, showed dramatic events in Princess Moo's life. The fiery Le Plongeon was furious at the icy attitude of his critics, but his sarcastic attacks by way of reply did not help his cause.

After his death in 1908 Alice Le Plongeon guarded his field notes, and when she herself was dying she confided to a friend that on one of their trips they had discovered a cache of Maya treasures. They had left the treasure safe in an underground hiding place. Now she could reveal it. The notes her friend jotted down in this emotional death-bed scene were unreadable later. The supposed treasure-trove would be secret forever.

Le Plongeon was not the most eccentric or aggressive of the many amateur excavators and writers whose off-beat theories drew public attention to the Atlantis legend during the nineteenth century. He was just one of dozens who protested—in his case at the top of his lungs—that individual "revelations" were more dependable than the dull, methodical work of the trained scientist. The campaign to make Atlantis "the source of all civilizations" was in full swing.

By the end of the nineteenth century the Atlantis legend was enjoying a popularity unmatched at any other time in its career. It had become a sort of folk religion, a cult with millions of believers. All things considered, it's surprising that P. T. Barnum never thought of putting real, live "Atlanteans" on display.

On the crest of the wave rode an American, Ignatius Donnelly. He wrote so engagingly about Atlantis that the age-old dream of locating and exploring that lost island seemed close to fulfillment. His enthusiasm was contagious. It was hard *not* to believe him.

Atlantis never had a champion of his stature before, and there has been none to equal him since.

IX

Crusader for Atlantis

His friends and his enemies alike would have laughed at the idea that Ignatius Donnelly might become an expert on the subject of Atlantis. All the time that he was preparing to do exactly that, he kept it to himself.

When he left his home town of Philadelphia in 1856, he was taking his bride, Katharine, to the wide-open territory of Minnesota. Frontier land was cheap. A man could build his own future on it. Only twenty-five, Donnelly was blessed with what his Irish forebears called the gift of gab. This peppery young lawyer could tame rowdy audiences with his oratory. He wrote just as persuasively. Atlantis, as yet, wasn't in his thoughts.

With several partners he organized a cooperative farm project that soon attracted settlers. A hotel was built and a newspaper edited by Donnelly started off with a flourish. What they worked toward would be something new under the prairie sun: a planned utopia.

But it could not weather the bank crash and panic of 1857. Their last chance for survival depended on the coming of the railroad, long awaited and long delayed. When the tracks were laid the trains bypassed their town by many miles. The hotel closed, the newspaper was done for, and the settlers departed. Nininger City, as they called their farming community, became a ghost town.

Donnelly was not one to weep over spilled milk, even if it came from cows bred on his own land. When Minnesota was made a state in 1859 he went into politics. Those talents he had for writing and public speaking hurried him on his way. First he became the new state's lieutenant governor and by 1862 he was in Washington, a duly elected member of the House of Representatives.

To the Honorable Ignatius Donnelly, people and ideas, politics and poetry, but not least of all, history—these were nearly as dear to him as his wife Katharine. Every expectation and disappointment of his was hers as well.

At this time the Atlantis legend entered his life. From one point of view it might be said that *he* entered *its* life. Uncountable hours of his free time were spent in the reading rooms of the Library of Congress. He was not poring over law books or Congressional bills; he was avidly studying everything he could find about Atlantis and its history. The magnitude of the subject appealed to his vigorous, problem-solving mind.

By now Donnelly had many political enemies, but none of them ever accused him of shirking his responsibilities. His quiet pursuit of Atlantis did not interfere with his work in the House. His enemies looked down their noses at him as a radical reformer because he wanted a system of public education broader than anything his colleagues thought sensible or prudent. As a lifelong foe of slavery he was a strong supporter of President Lincoln. This man Donnelly was such a flaming radical that he wanted women to have the right to vote.

His politics shifted with the years. After three terms as a Republican Congressman he was defeated and did newspaper work for a time. He spent another five years in the Minnesota Senate, but in 1878 he again lost his race for Congress when he ran as a Greenback-Democrat. Only then did he retire to write his first book. It made him famous. *Atlantis: The Antediluvian World* was a runaway success. Those hours in the Library of Congress were a sound investment. His own utopia had failed and saddled him with debts, but his book on the world's first utopia lifted that burden for good.

Thousands knew Donnelly as an independent in politics, and millions soon learned of him as the author of a book that charmed and amazed them. It spelled out his belief that Plato's story was history. He reasoned that if modern man would put his intellect and resources to the task, he could discover the rich ruins of Atlantis. Nations, he urged, should combine their naval fleets and search for it.

"This lost people were our ancestors," he wrote. "Their blood flows in our veins . . . the words we use every day were heard . . . in their cities, courts and temples."

He assured his spellbound readers that Atlantis was both the earliest and the greatest of the world's civilizations; every other culture was only an offshoot. Such statements went far beyond Plato's claims, *but how exciting it all was!*

The rediscovery of Atlantis appeared to be a matter of days or weeks away. First, England's Prime Minister William Gladstone extended cordial congratulations to

Mr. Donnelly. Then Mr. Gladstone implored the British Cabinet to contribute Treasury funds for the outfitting of a ship that would hunt for Atlantis. The Cabinet, less bemused than the Prime Minister, dragged its heels. No funds were provided, but news like this sent the sales of Donnelly's book skyrocketing.

Thanks to him, America and England fell in love with the Atlantis legend. Poets and editors wrote of it. Study clubs were formed and Donnelly's theories were discussed everywhere. Scarcely ten years earlier ancient Troy had been found. The man who unearthed its ruins, Heinrich Schliemann, had demonstrated that Troy was not merely a legend but a geographic place. And now, people wondered, would Atlantis be next? Why not?

With energy to burn, Donnelly enthusiastically lectured on the glories of Atlantis and hardly broke his stride to get back periodically into the hurly-burly of state politics. Twice he ran for the Vice-Presidency of the United States on the ticket of the new national People's Party, the Populists, as they were known. He was one of its founders. Audiences relished his wit and fluent arguments, whether he spoke for Atlantis or hammered away at the need for reforms in government and big business. Opponents said he was more wild-eyed than ever with his crazy political ideas. But his *book?* Well now, that was another matter!

The substance of his Atlantis theories is hinted at in its subtitle: *The Antediluvian World,* or the world before the flood. Donnelly said that the island of Atlantis was located in the Atlantic Ocean, opposite the mouth of the Mediterranean Sea. It was the remnant of an Atlantic continent and was ". . . known to the ancient world as Atlantis." Here man first rose from barbarism to civilization. When the island submerged, a few people escaped. They took their story and the seeds of their culture with them as they fled by ships and rafts.

The catastrophe became a memory common to all humanity, because the Atlanteans reached Europe and Africa, the West Indies and the Americas. Thus, Donnelly explained, Atlantis was the Garden of Eden of the Bible. It was Mount Olympus to the Greeks and the home of the Norse gods. Egyptian and Peruvian mythology ". . . represented the original religion of Atlantis, which was sun-worship." Greek gods were dim memories of Atlantean heroes.

The flood that drowned Atlantis is the happening behind every deluge and flood legend known, said Donnelly. All nations and all literature have such stories. And where might one expect to find its remains? He pointed to the Azores, those serenely beautiful islands in the North Atlantic. They were fragments of the land mass that sank 13,000 years ago. Once they were the cloud-covered mountain peaks of Atlantis, the same mountains that Plato said were ". . . higher and more beautiful than any that exist today." People consulted maps and read Plato, perhaps for the first time. *How logical Donnelly made it seem!*

Logical he was not, however. Donnelly had read Charles Étienne Brasseur. He reprinted Bishop Landa's alphabet, mistakes and all, to "prove" that the Maya language was derived from Latin. It is irresistible to think that, besides reading Le Plongeon, he had read Jules Verne. *Twenty Thousand Leagues Under the Sea* was published in an English edition in 1870.

Archaeology was a young science. The average person knew too little about it to be critical of Donnelly. He had the knack of making the intricate seem simple—provided one didn't check his sources or his statements too closely. What his readers gathered was that Atlantis could be rediscovered, and he promised that museums would someday display ". . . gems, statues, arms, and implements from Atlantis." Libraries would contain ". . . translations of the inscriptions on its sunken buildings." Shades of Captain Nemo and his underwater sightseeing tours!

According to Donnelly, that "great original race" invented gunpowder and paper. They were the first to manufacture iron and to make astronomy an exact science. All this knowledge they imparted to people less advanced than themselves. Egypt was one of their colonies. The Latin language, he said, evolved from the language spoken on the playing fields and in the markets of old Atlantis. What student struggling with Cicero or Caesar would not daydream about lost Atlantis?

Modern editions of *Atlantis: The Antediluvian World* are streamlined and heavily revised; whole sections have been scissored out and dropped. The reason is clear: Donnelly offered many theories as known and established facts that science did not support even then and wholly discredits today. He sidestepped or sometimes omitted details that would have contradicted his most telling arguments. Few readers had the background to judge what was historically incorrect in his book, what was archaeologically unsound, and how very much was imaginative guesswork.

Donnelly wrote other books, each on a different topic. One attempted to prove that Sir Francis Bacon was the author of the plays and poetry of William Shakespeare.

This was not a new theory, yet by advocating it warmly, Donnelly heated one more literary and historical controversy to a full boil. His crestfallen Atlantis fans felt that he had abandoned them.

He simply went his own way, occasionally returning to his rambling farmhouse in Nininger City to raise a few acres of wheat and start another book. Independent as always, Donnelly refused to look or act the part of a literary celebrity; he stayed defiantly clean-shaven when men in public life wore handsome beards. His stocky figure on the platform meant a full lecture hall whenever he spoke. Little known today as a crusader for social reform, Donnelly irritated and alarmed his political foes. They dubbed him "The Prince of Cranks."

Atlantis: The Antediluvian World has had more than fifty printings, one as recently as 1949, and the first paperback copies appeared in 1972. Some Atlantists continue to regard Donnelly as the supreme authority.

When he died in 1901 the legend lost its best-known champion. He had spread the gospel of romantic Atlantism far and wide. His social beliefs were ahead of his time. Donnelly was a fighter who recognized the need to conserve forested land in his own state. His drive to make education and the right to vote available to more and more people branded him a dangerous radical. Donnelly cared deeply about these issues, and he cared about Atlantis. This caring brought them to national attention.

Certain of his conservation and education measures went down to defeat in his lifetime but were written into law decades after his death. No credit accrued to him.

Prophet, visionary, radical reformer—Ignatius Donnelly gave years of dedicated service to his nation, and an equal share to the timeless legend.

X

Continents: Lost, Strayed, and Imaginary

❧ For all their wishing and hoping, the Atlantis hunters did not see their sparkling dream come true. The nineteenth century was drawing to its close, yet no sunken marble city was discovered and joyfully identified as Atlantis. Not even fragments were found of a rusty helmet or breastplate some Atlantean soldier might have worn in battle.

But the Atlantis seekers were not discouraged. By now they were calling themselves "Atlantists." Some of them preferred the title "Atlantologists," a word that hinted at impressive scholarship and learning. At meetings of their clubs and societies they mulled over the fate of lost tribes and lost continents. This kept them busy, because Atlantis was acquiring some new rivals.

One lost continent theory was launched during these

lively years by a German biologist, Ernst Haeckel. As a
supporter of Darwin's theory of evolution, Haeckel became curious about the lemur, a fuzzy little animal with
big eyes, a foxlike muzzle, and a bushy tail. It is related
to the monkey family though it is not classified as a true
monkey.

Only the disappearance of an entire continent in the
Indian Ocean could explain to Haeckel's satisfaction why
lemurs had managed to survive in places as far apart as
Africa, Malaysia, and India. A lost continent would account for their unusual distribution in the modern world.
Philip Sclater, a well-known English zoologist, agreed
with Haeckel and suggested the name "Lemuria" for the
absent land mass. Thus Lemuria has the distinction of
being the only continent named in honor of a monkey's
relative.

Any chance that it might be a threat to the popularity
of Atlantis seemed to end when the fossil forms of a great
many lemurs turned up in Europe and the Americas. The
competing theory of Lemuria keeled over and sank. But
it did not stay under for long.

Once they come into existence, lost continents do not
simply vanish. Lemuria lingers on. There are people today
who believe that the last of the Lemurians live deep
within beautiful Mount Shasta, a dormant volcano in
Northern California. Some say they have seen the strange
robed and silent Lemurians come down from their mountain and shop for canned goods in a nearby town. They
pay for their supplies with sacks of gold dust.

Whenever a lost continent is created, beings of superhuman intelligence put in an appearance sooner or later
to inhabit it. By some unwritten rule they are weird in

appearance and possessed of supernatural powers. So are their "descendants."

Another continent was proclaimed by James Church-ward, a retired Scottish army officer. His research was done in the late 1800s, that era of expansive promise, but he did not write about *his* continent until the 1920s. It was Churchward who shortened the word *Lemuria* to *Mu.* Incidentally, there is no direct connection between it and Le Plongeon's Queen Moo or Mu.

Churchward described his land as ". . . a large conti-nent situated in the Pacific Ocean between America and Asia." Its center was south of the equator. On Mu a glori-ous civilization reached its peak thirteen thousand years ago.

In his book, *The Lost Continent of Mu,* Churchward told of learning the history of Mu after he studied the writing on some stone tablets in Tibet. They were twelve thousand years old. For the benefit of skeptics, Church-ward explained that he could read the Muvian inscriptions as easily as he could read "all other languages." He had his intuition, not any training in languages, to guide him.

If the various lost continent theories were often in obvi-ous conflict with each other, it did not matter too much; the differences could somehow be reconciled. When dyed-in-the-wool Atlantologists objected to his upstart conti-nent, Churchward informed them that Atlantis had first been settled and civilized by missionary priests from Mu. Then a world-wide tragedy affected both lands. Exactly thirteen thousand years ago, so the stone tablets said, great caves beneath the surface of Mu and Atlantis collapsed. The two continents crumbled when these volcanic "gas-belts" gave way. Along with Mu, Atlantis slid below sea level, never to reappear.

Understandably, the Atlantologists didn't like any of this. But enough fresh recruits fell into step with Churchward to make his books sell briskly. They still can be had as paperbacks.

The creation of one more continent was the work of Lewis Spence, whose books also came out in the 1920s. The present traces of Antilia, his continent, are the Antilles Islands in the West Indies group.

Spence was actually reviving the popular fifteenth-century tradition of the legendary Antilia that was rectangular in shape and was shown on many old maps, including a navigational chart used by Columbus. Columbus's belief in a real Antilia made him hopeful of finding it on his westward course to the Indies.

Spence added a new wrinkle by proposing that Antilia was a land-bridge, at one time connecting the Americas with Atlantis. He generously positioned Atlantis in its classic spot, the Atlantic Ocean, and kept Lemuria in the Pacific. To wrap everything into one neat package, Spence had refugees from Atlantis settling first in Antilia, then migrating to Yucatán when Antilia sank. He traced the origins of the Maya culture to those uprooted early Atlanteans. To Spence, a Mexican Indian legend about the destruction of the old Toltec capital was a distorted memory of the Atlantis disaster.

Few of these theories got more than passing interest from serious scientists. But Atlantologists and those who believed in mysticism and the occult found them all fascinating.

There is this to be said for any lost continent: it is as

difficult to make a case for its previous existence as to prove that it never existed. A creative mind can endow a lost continent with its own geography, history, and folklore, then let it sink without a trace. There is no argument with the imagination. That is essentially what Aristotle said about Plato's Atlantis thousands of years ago.

Something else can be said for such theories. Men like Le Plongeon, Churchward, Spence—and heading the list, Donnelly—these men were mythmakers. Each of them had an influence on the Atlantis legend, helping to keep it perennially fresh and controversial. Their versions of history were faulty, their scientific "facts" foggy and unprovable. But Plato's story had to be reckoned with because the mythmakers dragged it in and volunteered their own interpretations of it.

Le Plongeon and Spence were quick to defend their extreme claims by saying that they had personal gifts of "intuition." Spence spoke mockingly of the systematic work of field and laboratory scientists. "The Tape-Measure School," he called it, setting it apart from the "inspiration" that was his guide. Both Spence and Le Plongeon bid for sympathy from their followers by accusing "jealous" scientists of ignoring and slighting them. To argue with a man's inspiration is just as futile as to argue with his imagination.

While the battle raged, Atlantis continued to be the most mysterious and charming of any lost land imaginable.

XI

"I Have Discovered Atlantis!"

In the fall of 1912, readers of the New York *American* unfolded their Sunday newspapers and were greeted by these eye-catching headlines:

HOW I FOUND THE LOST ATLANTIS, THE SOURCE OF ALL CIVILIZATION

This thunderclap announcement was made by a man whose name had a teasingly familiar ring to it. Thus did Dr. Paul Schliemann break the news that an English expedition had recently set forth to probe the ocean floor for traces of Atlantis. He introduced himself as a grandson of the famous Heinrich Schliemann, the archaeologist who discovered the ruins of ancient Troy in 1873.

The magic of the Schliemann name and the science-fiction tone of his article persuaded many readers that the long-awaited day of discovery was dawning. For a brief while Atlantis enjoyed the gaudiest publicity it had known since the days of Ignatius Donnelly.

"I have discovered Atlantis!" Schliemann wrote. *"I have verified the existence of this great continent and the fact that from it sprang all the civilizations of historic times."*

His narrative included a touching deathbed scene, a standard item in many tales of treasure hunting. According to the grandson's account, when the archaeologist was digging at Troy he came upon a bronze vase decorated with an owl's head. The Phoenician words "From the King Chronos of Atlantis" were engraved on it. He kept this find a secret from everyone, his nearest and dearest alike. A few days before his death he sent it in a package together with a sealed envelope to a close friend. These words were on the envelope:

> *"This can be opened only by a member of my family who solemnly vows to devote his life to the researches outlined therein."*

Barely an hour before his death, he had a nurse deliver a second message to the friend. This was labeled "Confidential addition to the sealed envelope."

Paul Schliemann said he was reluctant to assume such a heavy responsibility. After studying in Russia, Germany, and the Orient (exactly what, he did not say), he unsealed the envelopes. The first paper he read required him to take that solemn vow to carry on *the unfinished work of searching for Atlantis.* He so swore. Other documents consisted of clues collected by his grandfather.

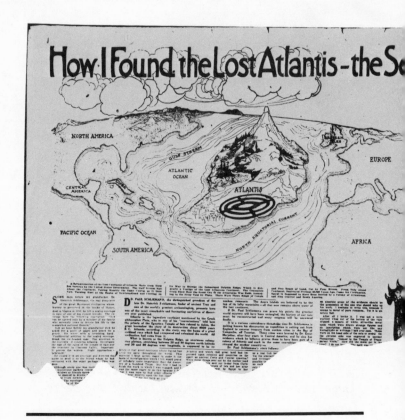

How I Found the Lost Atlantis – the S...

SOME days before my grandfather Dr. Heinrich Schliemann, the most famous archaeologist of the great Mycenaean civilization whose history is preserved in the books of Homer, died in Naples in 1890 he left a sealed envelope in care of one of his closest friends. The envelope bore these words: "This can be opened only by a member of my family who solemnly vows to devote his life to the researches outlined therein."

Just an hour before my grandfather he asked for a piece of paper and pencil in his pencil. He wrote with a trembling hand "Confidential addition to the sealed envelope. Break the re-sealed case. Pay attention to the contents. It concerns Atlantis. Investigate the east of the ruins of the temple of Sais and the cemetery in Chacuna Valley. Important. It proves the subject. Night approaches — Schliemann."

He closed it in an envelope and directed the nurse to send it to his friend whom he had entrusted with the other package. This was done.

Although every one may not discover the mysterious symbols which were hidden or hidden in the family relics it was not destined to discover his life before his eyes there...

The mysterious...

D PAUL SCHLIEMANN, the distinguished grandson of the late Dr. Heinrich Schliemann, finder of ancient Troy and one of the world's greatest archaeologists, presents here one of the most remarkable and fascinating narratives of discovery ever published.

Atlantis is the legendary continent mentioned by the Greek philosopher Plato, who is one of his "conversations" told how the priests of the Egyptian Temple of Sais related to Solon, the great lawmaker the story of its destruction about 9000 years B. C. Atlantis, according to this story, was the home of a great civilized race which had conquered and colonized the world. All civilization had come from it.

What is known as the Dolphin Ridge, an enormous submarine plateau, stretching between 25 and 50 degrees north latitude and 20 and 80 degrees west longitude, is supposed to be the...

[columns of text continue, largely illegible]

Next, said Paul Schliemann, he broke the vase. Out spilled bits of pottery, small images, objects made of fossilized bone, and one coin of a silverlike metal he could not identify.

Anyone with the scantiest knowledge of Heinrich Schliemann's career would have found several of these actions highly uncharacteristic of the man. He did not shy away from publicity, and seldom was he reticent about discussing any theories he held or discoveries he made.

Again, one needed to know little about geography to

The newspaper article shown reads, in part:

of All Civilization.

By Dr. Paul Schliemann,

Grandson of Dr. Heinrich Schliemann, Who Discovered and Excavated Ancient Troy and Other Great Cities of the Mycenaean Civilization, Which Preceded and Was Greater Than That of the Greeks.

...onishing Scientific Narrative Ever Published the Grandson of Troy's ...ells Why He Believes He Has Unravelled the Greatest World Mystery

What the Lost Atlantis Is Supposed to Have Been.

The article by Paul Schliemann appearing in N.Y. American, *October, 1912.* (Courtesy of Microfilm Archives, University of Texas.)

be surprised by statements in letters that Paul Schliemann published as his grandfather's writings. In one of them the archaeologist spoke of excavating "at the Lion Gate at Mycenae in Crete."

Now, Mycenae is an ancient city on the Greek Peloponnesus, a considerable distance from the *island* of Crete. It is a historic fact that Heinrich Schliemann worked at Mycenae; in one area of its ruined acropolis he uncovered the shaft graves of Bronze Age nobles. But he was incapable of making such an error in geography. Sick, well, or on his deathbed, Heinrich Schliemann would not have placed Mycenae on Crete.

The article rambled its way from Central America to Greece and from England to the African coast as Paul Schliemann recounted the journeys he took to carry out the dead man's instructions. He was looking for objects to match those in the owl vase. By a lucky chance "an Egyptian hunter"—not otherwise identified—showed him coins taken from the sarcophagus of a First Dynasty priest; they were duplicates of the one in the owl vase. Tests proved that their metal was an alloy of platinum, aluminum, and silver.

In Central America he found another coin like them. A second owl vase, also containing a coin, was found among some South American art objects in the collection of a private owner.

French geographers helped him explore the coast of West Africa. More "secret evidence" came to light. His six years of research were financed by a fund his grandfather had thoughtfully deposited for that purpose in the Bank of France.

At last Paul Schliemann had evidence that the continent of Atlantis once touched Africa, as his grandfather had suspected. At this and other crucial points in his narrative, he declined to go into detail about the evidence, promising instead to reveal the whole story later. He was writing a book that would clarify everything. And the world, he said, would be astonished by his revelations.

Some of his literary research drew upon "a Maya manuscript which is part of the famous collection of Le Plongeon." One passage he quoted described the sinking of Mu in Central America, a translation made by Dr. Le Plongeon. An incredibly old Chaldean manuscript was another lucky find. This foretold the destruction of "the land of Seven Cities" by earthquake and eruption. Presumably this meant Atlantis, and Mu was Atlantis, too— though a reader could not be blamed for feeling befuddled. The Mu-Atlantis connection was not clear. Much was not clear. Well-informed Atlantologists recognized "the land of Seven Cities" as an obscure reference to lost Antilia, but that only added to the confusion.

Assured that his task was finished, Paul Schliemann summed up his conclusions:

—The owl vase found at Troy was evidence that one of the earliest Trojan settlements had been a colony of Atlantis.

—Atlantis once connected "what we now call the New World with what we call the old."

—The coins in the owl vases, like those from Egypt and Central America, had been the common currency of Atlantis and her colonies. Egypt, Peru, and Central America were colonial powers founded and fostered by Atlantis.

—The religions of the colonies featured sun worship; all were derived from the original religion of Atlantis.

—The Atlanteans fully understood electricity and steam. They had airplanes and power-driven ships.

As to the present location of Atlantis, Paul Schliemann said unequivocally that the Azores Islands were the tips of its submerged mountains.

Not once did he mention Ignatius Donnelly, although he used that writer's words to call Atlantis "the cradle of civilization." Again—no credit given—he borrowed many of Donnelly's ideas, including the concept that the classic Greek gods were "racial memories" of Atlantean nobles and heroes.

Readers who waited anxiously for further news had a

long, long wait. If that English expedition did reach its goal and sent divers down to explore the sea floor, no reports were made of their findings.

Was Paul Schliemann's book a success? If it was written, it was not published.

What about the owl vases, the coins, the secret documents from the hand of Heinrich Schliemann? If they existed, they were not made available for study.

Dr. Wilhelm Dörpfeld was the distinguished scientist who had worked closely with Heinrich Schliemann in the last years of his career, a valued and trusted friend. Shortly after the publication of this article, Dr. Dörpfeld was asked to comment about the archaeologist's concern with Atlantis. His dignified response was that to the best of his knowledge the subject had not interested Schliemann, nor had he done any research on it.

Nothing more appeared over the signature of Paul Schliemann in magazines or newspapers, either about his grandfather or Atlantis. The whole story had struck the more reflective Atlantologists as being much too good to be true. The fact is that Heinrich Schliemann did not have a grandson named Paul.

XII

They Looked on Wonders

When John Lloyd Stephens climbed aboard the brig *Mary Ann* in New York's North River, he carried the credentials of an American diplomat. This was in 1839, shortly after President Van Buren had offered him a confidential mission to Central America. Stephens had accepted promptly.

Nobody envied him the appointment. The four men who had held the post of envoy before him had died in office. Stephens was a lawyer of thirty-two. He was still surprised to find himself suddenly famous because of two books he had written. But he was a man to take success in stride, a bit amused and very gratified. The truth was that he much preferred travel and writing to the practice of law.

The books were entertaining accounts of his travels

in Egypt, Greece, and Arabia. Critics thought highly of them and the public loved them. Then why, people wondered, should he want this secret mission to godforsaken Central America? The land had been in political turmoil for years.

Stephens had a secret of his own. Diplomacy didn't interest him, but he was relying on his new official status to smooth his way, because the real and overriding purpose of the trip was to explore for ruined cities in the jungles. Various travelers had published reports of seeing "Egyptian" pyramids in Mexico and Guatemala. Some described the ruins of palaces that looked "unmistakably" Carthaginian or Phoenician. Stephens intended to see these for himself. He said that he was going "with the hope, rather than expectation, of finding wonders."

His formal duties were routine. He was to locate the representatives of something called the Central American Republic—if they could be found. Then he would close the American legation and get a trade treaty signed—if possible. It was an ideal way of combining state business with exploration.

Stephens was acting on a plan made three years earlier with Frederick Catherwood, an English artist, when they met in London. Catherwood himself was now on board the *Mary Ann*. In lieu of diplomatic credentials he was taking paper, pencils, brushes, pigments, and some surveyor's instruments.

This young artist shared John Stephens's passion for exploring. He was an architect and draftsman who had sketched and painted his way through Europe and the Near East for years. Meeting Stephens led to the discovery that they had the same intense feeling of wonder about the buildings and monuments of vanished civilizations. To join Stephens in the search for strange ruins was an opportunity Catherwood seized without a second thought. This journey of theirs was inevitable.

They left in October for Belize, the port in British Honduras that was their point of departure for the wild interior of Guatemala.

These two men, without fanfare or heroics, actually laid the groundwork for American archaeology. They rediscovered the forgotten world of the Maya. Neither claimed to be more than what he was, the one a journalist, the other an artist. That they were amateur archaeologists of talent and insight was a happenstance, and a fortunate one.

It was true of them as of others whose work shaped history: they brought about changes in the Atlantis legend. This outcome would not be evident for years and was accidental, never a part of their thoughts or plans.

In 1839, the world was so ignorant of the Maya that even their name was forgotten. Bishop Landa's book was still "lost," like many writings of the Conquest period. The dominant theory about all Indians made them descendants of the Lost Tribesmen of ancient Israel. This curious belief continued to prevail as it had for two hundred years, seldom questioned by historians or clergy. It did get opposition from those who clung with equal earnestness to the idea that the ancestors of America's Indians had come from Atlantis. These never-say-die believers held fast to their faith that the Indians were Atlanteans, not Jews.

Quaint as the argument may seem today, it was a serious matter. It stayed in the realm of controversy as long

as the ruined sites themselves were unexplored and un-
identified.

And now came Stephens and Catherwood, eager to see
the disputed ruins with their own eyes. They had puzzled
over a set of lavish art books published by Edward King
and titled *The Antiquities of Mexico*. King was a young
Irish nobleman who held the formal title of Viscount
Kingsborough. He sank his fortune into the publication
of these books. Their theme, again, was that the Indians
were "Semites."

King's venture began after he saw an Aztec painted
book in a British museum. He called it *Mexican,* using the
word that historians of the day gave to any art form native
to Latin America. Then he hired artists to make hand-
colored copies of all the painted books scattered throughout Europe. The project ended in disaster. In 1837 Edward
King died in debtor's prison, owing money to the firm that
manufactured the paper for his books. Not quite two years
later, Stephens and Catherwood set out on their journey.

A month after leaving New York, they were making
their way by muleback over treacherous mountain trails
toward Guatemala City. The country was in the ferment
of civil war. They came prepared for the discomforts of
travel, but not for the highhanded treatment of petty officials. Once a drunk officer locked them in the town jail.
Stephens' flair for diplomacy was put to its first test. They
were released and went on to the village of Copán, in
Honduras, one of several places where ancient ruins had
been reported.

At first, even to their trained eyes, there was nothing
to see. But what they eventually discovered at Copán,
almost wholly concealed by deep-rooted trees and lush

vines, was an ancient city on the grand scale. Stephens
bought the site for fifty dollars, and they worked with
native guides for two weeks to hack and strip away enough
of the heavy overgrowth to uncover the architectural plan
of the entire city. Courts, pyramids, and terraces of carved
stonework were laid open to view. The complex of buildings was so vast that for a time they moved about like
men in a dream. Stone jaguar heads and figures of unknown gods emerged from the jungle foliage, seeming to
peer at them ominously while they inched their way
through the desolate site.

One imposing stairway was encrusted with carved hieroglyphs. Stephens gave it his most scrupulous attention.
It struck him that this peculiar writing was the clue to
the city's history and its builders. His surmise was both
brilliant and correct, as time would show. He and Catherwood could not help asking who had built all this, and
when, and for what purpose. The only reply from their
guides was «¿Quien sabe?»—Who knows?

John Lloyd Stephens was gazing on wonders, but he
knew he must look for answers to the questions they pro-
voked.

Catherwood made drawings of individual buildings and
prepared a master plan of the city. He often worked wearing gloves to ward off clouds of mosquitoes, and he
worked in good weather or drenching, steamy rain, moving from one ruined structure to another. He concentrated
also on eleven stone stelae—figures bearing elaborate
hieroglyphs. His drawings were accurate to the finest,
most intricate detail. He agreed with Stephens that the
savage beauty of the Copán ruins had nothing in common
with Egyptian architecture, which he knew well. These

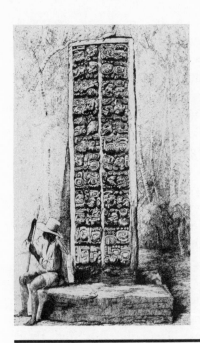

Figure 29: *Stone Idol at Copán.* (From *Incidents of Travel in Yucatán*, by John Lloyd Stephens. New edition copyright 1962 by University of Oklahoma Press.)

were the creation of a people native to the land, artistic, inventive, and unknown. His drawings captured both the grandeur of the buildings and the spirit of their decorative art. Nothing at Copán resembled the classical buildings he had studied in the Mediterranean world.

Stephens left for Guatemala to look for the government officials to whom he was supposed to present himself and his papers, but he never located them. The government had simply ceased to exist. For the occasion he had brought along a splendid blue jacket with gold buttons, made to his order in New York. He had to write it off as "a dead loss." So was the diplomatic mission. His time was now his own, and back he went to Copán.

Not before Catherwood completed the many drawings

Plate 29: *House of the Nuns* (monjas), *Chichén Itzá*
(From *Incidents of Travel in Yucatán,* by John Lloyd Stephens. New edition copyright 1962 by University of Oklahoma Press.)

he wanted did they quit the site to head for Mexico and the ruins of Palenque, in Chiapas. They saw at once how similar Palenque's architecture was to Copán's. Could this be coincidence? Something more was known about this ruined city than any other. A people called the Maya had built it. Three hundred miles separated the two cities, and Stephens drew the only inference possible. Then, at Uxmal in Yucatán, any last doubts left him. Here again were the same types of buildings, the same daring feats of engineering, the same unreadable hieroglyphs. *The builders were the Maya!*

Their journey was cut short when Stephens suddenly became ill and returned to New York.

Copán had been like the slow lifting of a heavy curtain

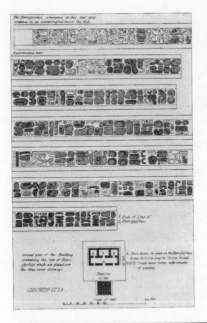

Plate 33: *Heiroglyphs at Chichén Itzá.* (From *Incidents of Travel in Yucatán,* by John Lloyd Stephens. New edition copyright 1962 by University of Oklahoma Press.)

that had hidden the Maya from the modern world. They were lost no longer. The journalist and the artist had rediscovered them.

Ill or not, Stephens wrote a book about their journey that appeared in 1841 as *Incidents of Travel in Central America, Chiapas and Yucatán.* It was illustrated by Catherwood, who supervised the artwork while his drawings were made into woodcuts and engravings, though all the while he was suffering from malaria. This unwelcome gift of the jungle later attacked Stephens. He never completely recovered from it.

Their work charted the new direction that archaeology took in the Americas. One critic said of their book that it was ". . . among the foremost achievements of Ameri-

Plate 34: *Gymnasium at Chichén Itzá.* (From *Incidents of Travel in Yucatán,* by John Lloyd Stephens. New edition copyright 1962 by University of Oklahoma Press.)

can literature." Indeed, it became an American classic, unexpectedly as popular as it was influential. There was laughter in its pages, and human drama, but when Stephens gave his incisive and reasoned views of the Maya achievement, he was an eloquent spokesman for a people bypassed by an accident of history. He wrote:

> "*Unless I am wrong, we have a conclusion far more interesting and wonderful than that of connecting the builders of these cities with the Egyptians or any other people. It is the spectacle of a people skilled in architecture, sculpture, and drawing, and beyond doubt, other more perishable arts, and possessing the cultivation and refinement attendant upon these, not*

*derived from the Old World, but originating and
growing here without models or masters, having a
distinct, separate, and independent existence; like
the plants and fruits of the soil, indigenous."*

Additional discoveries were made on their second journey, beginning in 1841. Altogether they found and explored forty-four Maya cities, many of them not known
before.

How did their teamwork alter the life story of the
Atlantis legend? Except for those whom neither logic nor
tangible evidence could budge, they had settled the dis-
pute about the builders of these soaring pyramids and
terraced courts. Professional archaeologists followed their
blazed trails to the sites, to establish once and for all that
their inspiration had not come from China, Egypt, Car-
thage, or from any lost continent, including Plato's kingdom of Atlantis.

Stephens and Catherwood dealt blow after blow to
every theory that placed Atlantis in the Americas with the
easy claim that the majestic Maya cities had been built by
exiled Atlanteans. From now on the legend was no longer
secure in its New World setting. These two explorers were
concerned with the provable truth. If they had not done
their work so well, Brasseur and Le Plongeon would probably have attracted much larger followings. Ignatius Donnelly himself did not attempt to anchor Atlantis in America, although he did enchant millions of readers with his
vision of the lost land found and reclaimed for the en-
lightenment of all mankind.

Archaeologists regard John Lloyd Stephens as the pio-
neer in Maya discoveries. He is to them "el padre del

Mayismo"—the father of Maya studies. They have also a special appreciation for Catherwood's drawings, whose value the years enhance. Time has damaged and vandals marred some of the monuments and buildings his pictures preserve. They have a special value today to those working on the decipherment of Maya writing. The symbols and figures he did not understand are vividly clear. They are as clear now as they were to his discerning eye when the jungle growth was first stripped away and the sunlight fell once more on the carved inscriptions of a people who for a while had lost their own name.

XIII

A Canal and a Volcano

In Plato's original story, it was no trouble at all for the god Poseidon to carve rings of water on Atlantis. But for the kings who followed him, it took many years to build canals near their capital city, even though they were still partly divine.

Pity the French engineers who began work on the Suez Canal in 1859! They were entirely mortal. Dozens of problems faced them. An urgent one was the need to locate plentiful supplies of cement for a canal one hundred miles long. It had to be of highest quality, not too distant or costly to transport by freighter.

What in the world has the Suez Canal to do with the legend of Atlantis? At first glance, nothing. A longer look reveals that there is an unlikely but direct connection. The engineers' requirements for cement led to the discovery of some ancient buried ruins on an island in the Aegean Sea. Their importance was not fully appreciated at the time. As a result, the published reports of the discovery were all but forgotten for a century. Yet it was these ruins that eventually brought the legend back from its adventurous trip to the Americas and home to its native Greece.

But this part of the Atlantis story deserves to be told just as it happened.

The French found their source of cement on Thera (now known as Santorini), an island sixty miles north of Crete. It was unbelievably rich in volcanic ash and pumice, as deep as a hundred and fifty feet in places. Mining it was easy. Large masses were pried loose and spilled down the cliffsides in chutes, for loading into ships below. When the white ash was mixed with lime it made an excellent waterproof cement, durable and cheap.

The name Thera actually applies to the largest of a cluster of little islands and to the entire cluster as well. From an airplane they look like a broken circle, thirty square miles in size. Far in the past they were a single island called Kallistë, meaning "Most Beautiful Island." Another of its ancient names was Strongulê, "Circular Island." Then it was changed to Thera. According to tradition, this was done when Theras, a conqueror from Sparta, took it over in the ninth century B.C. What is worth noting is that by that time *the once round island had become a group.* Theras bestowed his name on the largest of them and on the group as a whole.

The name-shuffling went on. During the Middle Ages, when Venice ruled these waters, Thera became Santorini, or as the French call it, Santorin, in honor of Saint Irene, its patron saint. Scientists who are concerned with its human and geological history today usually refer to it as Thera, and the word includes the entire cluster.

Close to the crescent-shaped main island and a little to the west lies Therasia. Tiny Aspronsi is southwest, its cliffs covered with layers of white ash. In the center of the inner bay are the Kameni, the "Burnt Islands." They are aptly named, because they sputter and steam with volcanic activity. They are the vents of the old volcano, which is gradually rebuilding itself. The bay itself is so deep that sailors say it has no bottom; measurements put its depth at twelve hundred feet.

Phirá is a village of neat white buildings on the largest island. It stands atop the highest cliffs, eleven hundred feet above the water. Tourists who arrive by ship have their choice of going by foot or donkeyback on the road that zigzags its way dizzily up the side of the steep cliff to Phirá, the main town. Fishing and open-air pumice mining are the Therans' livelihood, aside from the summer tourist trade. At best it is a meager livelihood, even in years when the vineyards bear good harvests of wine grapes. Tomatoes, fava beans, and bar'ey are other staple crops.

Thera was and still is an active volcano. Many centuries ago it erupted with such violence that the upper part of its great volcanic mountain exploded. This happened after volcanic matter from a deep undersea chamber was discharged as pumice and ash. Once emptied, the lower structure became a hollow void. The volcano, now only the shell of a mountain, blew apart. The center of the circular island was blown high in the air, then fell back and was swept downward. The boiling sea rushed in to fill

The zigzag donkey trail as seen from the caldera. Town of Phirá above. (Photograph by Mary A. Cowden.)

---

the great void. Scientists call such a crater a *caldera,* or "cauldron." Far below sea level the old volcano still works without ceasing.

Thera's gaunt cliffs rise like uneven walls over the deep water of the caldera. They are the ancient crater's rim. Crater Lake in Oregon resembles Thera in several respects; it too is a caldera whose shape was forged by a now extinct volcano.

The forces of destruction have left scars everywhere. The cliffs that were once the mighty shoulders of a mountain are torn and severed. Layers of ash and pumice run horizontally through Thera's cliffsides in ribbonlike bands of color. Much of the ash is white, some reddish-yellow or gray. Volcanic pumice, which is equally valuable as material for cement, is visible as bands of pink. Occa-

A close-up view of Thera's scarred cliffs and the town of Phirá. (Photograph by Mary Alice Keir.)

sionally it too is gray or white and occurs in pieces the size of big pebbles. Coarser than ash, it is porous enough to float. All these layers are supported by massive segments of upthrust black and brown lava. They are the oldest rock, the bedrock of the island. The displaced strata and deep layering of pumice and ash testify to the terrible power unleashed by a volcanic convulsion more powerful than any in recorded history.

When did that eruption take place? Did it happen in stages, perhaps over a long period of time, or all at once? A hundred years ago it was impossible to name any date at all for a terrifying natural disaster.

Whenever it happened, the eruption did not destroy the volcano itself. Hot lava went on seeping from vents on the sea floor. In the second century B.C. the first of the

Town of Phirá, looking south. Pumice quarry is to the right. (Photograph by Mary Alice Keir.)

Burnt Islands pushed above the surface of the bay.

During the past two thousand years Thera has experienced other eruptions, but none so intense. Earthquakes are frequent. Many people were killed in a 1956 earthquake. But nothing compares with the catastrophe that reduced "Most Beautiful Island" to ash-strewn fragments.

Regardless of what the Suez Canal builders might have thought of Thera's unearthly appearance, to them it was just a cement mine. By the mid-1860s shiploads of material were shuttling to the canal site from two mines on Therasia and one on Thera.

In 1866 the volcano rumbled back to life. Loud explosions were accompanied by clouds of vapor. Hot lava was pushing up from the depths and pouring from a brand new cone in the Kameni.

The Greek government sent a commission of scientists to record its activity. French officials stationed a geologist named Ferdinand Fouqué at Thera as their own observer. His specialty was volcanology, but his scientific interests were broad and far-ranging. Fouqué had been drawn to geology three years after receiving his degree in medicine. He came to Thera from Italy, where he had been making studies of the erupting Vesuvius.

He found that work had recently halted at Therasia's southern mine because the workmen had struck so many stone blocks beneath the ash that they interfered with mining operations. The blocks had been cut by human hands; anyone could tell that by looking at them. *They lay a hundred feet below the layers of ash.*

Like the owner of the property and the Greek officials, Fouqué thought that the blocks were the remains of house walls. How had they come to be so deeply buried? Which had been present first, the volcanic rubble or the hand-hewn walls? Finding bits and pieces of ruins was such an old story to the miners that they weren't very interested in them. Fortunately, the visiting Greek scientists thought the walls deserved closer study. So did Fouqué.

Dangerous as it was to work in the mine area, where tons of ash could slip and suffocate a man, he joined the others in tracing the walls. They soon agreed that the blocks had been set in place before the pumice and ash showered down on them. What they found next was a complete surprise: the ruins of a six-room farmhouse. Because they had been sealed away from air and rain for untold centuries, the furniture and pottery in its rooms were well preserved. They were primitive in style but of an age or period in history no one among them could recognize.

Fouqué, who led the excavation of this house, kept detailed field notes. One section described the walls. They were lava blocks held together with clay mortar and reinforced with olivewood beams that still had bark on them. There were stairs, a hall with columns, and windows that faced the sea. A skeleton in one room was that of an old man who was crushed to death when the room gave way. This was the first hint that the eruption had taken its toll in human suffering.

The excavation went slowly. It was hazardous. Fouqué had seen evidence that there were ruins like these in shallower ash-deposits near Akrotiri, a village on the main island. He tried to buy land here, where he could work at less peril, because he was positive that what lay beneath the ash was historically valuable and significant. From a footpath near a ravine that rain had eroded and channeled, he could see, just over his head, thousands of pottery fragments and oddly tilted walls embedded in the ash. He dug at one spot for a couple of hours. It took him no longer than that to pry loose the shards of several vases. Later he pieced them together. In another nearby ravine were two golden rings.

But Fouqué was unable to reach an agreement with the owner on a selling price for the land. No matter; he went on examining and testing this region of Thera's southern coast, where the banks of ash were relatively thin from long exposure to the weather. Rain-swollen streams had cut deeply into the cliffsides.

To Fouqué these discoveries had no precedent. Everything he had seen was unfamiliar. From all indications the ruins were much older than Pompeii, the Roman city smothered by volcanic ash during an eruption of Vesuvius in 79 A.D. What lay under Thera's ash belonged to a prehistoric period that neither he nor anyone else could identify.

There was a reason for his uncertainty. Sir Arthur Evans did not excavate the Palace of Minos at Knossos, on Crete, until the early 1900s—thirty years in the future. Before he did, nothing was known about the existence of the brilliant Minoan culture, a Bronze Age civilization. That is why Fouqué classified the Thera ruins as "pre-Greek." But it was now perfectly clear to him that the island had been settled long before the great eruption.

The Greek observers departed, their mission ended. By 1870 Fouqué's assignment was also drawing to a close. He made a strong appeal to his colleagues at the French School of Archaeology in Athens, urging them to continue the excavations. He was heard. In April two men arrived at Thera who were ready to carry forward the work with the aid of a French government grant.

After Fouqué left, the rest of his distinguished professional life was given over to field work, teaching, and research. He made important contributions to the scientific understanding of volcanoes and the mineral by-products of their eruptions.

The newcomers to Thera were Mamet, a graduate student in archaeology, and Gorceix (pronounced Gor SAY), his fellow student, who was specializing in geology. They were young men and enthusiastic about their unexpected opportunity. In less than two months they were destined, like John Lloyd Stephens at Copán, to find wonders.

XIV

Under the Ash, a New Pompeii

The narrow southern tip of Thera was the area they chose for intensive excavation. In Fouqué's judgment it would be the most fruitful place to work. The volcano still thundered at regular intervals and spurted jets of vapor high in the air. Twice in 1867 the islanders had been terrified when sulfurous fumes from new cones in the Kameni mingled with heavy rainfall. A humid, noxious mist drifted across parts of the main island, badly damaging their vineyards. In four years the size of the Kameni had increased four-fold. But the worst was over. The volcano was entering a quiet phase.

Although Mamet and Gorceix were hopeful of success, they were realistic; it would not come overnight. Yet as early as May they were reporting "happy results surpassing our hopes."

The first of many impressive finds was made south of Akrotiri at a site discovered earlier by Fouqué, who had done some preliminary digging there. A three-room house was buried under pumice. Its walls were of quarried stone, some of them six feet high, on the edge of the cliff over-looking the bay. The rooms contained a variety of house-hold wares—simple cooking pots and pitchers along with well-fashioned painted vases.

As shown on the plan drawn by Mamet, one room con-tained an inner partition, R. They were trying to clear debris away from it when they broke through a wall. It opened into an underground passage roofed by a vault of pumice. The least shock could disturb the fragile vault, but they dared to enter and made their way cautiously along the tunnel that ran through and under a steep, sloping bank of gravel and pumice twelve feet thick. They were beneath a vineyard!

One wall of the passage, E, was coated with white plaster and bore the traces of a fresco painting. They had seen nothing like it. A few paces farther and they reached an opening in the wall. It was the doorway, H, of a larger room to the right of the tunnel. Pieces of its wooden door were easy to recognize.

They saw that the wall opposite them, F, as they paused in the doorway, was covered with bright fresco designs in bold, clear colors of earth and sky. Graceful red flowers like long-stemmed lilies stood out against the white back-ground. Bands of red, yellow, brown, and a vibrant shade of blue formed the lower border of the painting.

For an instant it seemed to the astonished men that time stood still. But as they watched, the colors began to fade when currents of air reached them.

That incredible vision told them they were in a dwelling more like a villa than any farmhouse or peasant hut. Fragments of painted plaster on the floors suggested that the ceilings of other rooms had been painted.

The excavators were able to remove scores of vases in good condition before they decided, regretfully, that they would have to abandon the house. The unstable bank overhead made further work too precarious. A sixth sense must have informed them, because a cave-in occurred soon after they stopped. The frescoes were buried, no doubt shattered, under tons of rubble.

Mamet's plan of this "House of Frescoes" shows that

Plan of the House of Frescoes drawn by Mamet. Modern foot-path (chemin) leads past the house.

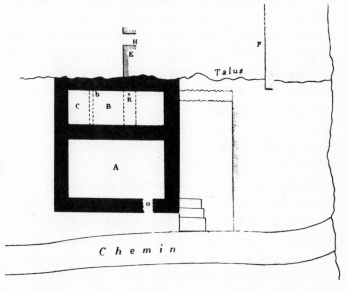

besides a cellar and stairway, it had a drainage system, b, which channeled rainwater from the roof to an indoor cistern. A break in one wall, o, was at first thought to be the main entrance, but they decided later that a landslide had caused it.

Like John Lloyd Stephens, having begun with hope rather than expectation, Mamet and Gorceix had found wonders. These young men of science were intensely moved by the overwhelming evidence that they were exploring human habitations of dignity and beauty too old to have any known place in history. They located other buildings that could be opened with less difficulty and were constantly amazed by the amount of furniture and pottery in them. Sometimes they found pieces of woven fabric.

It was Fouqué who first called the ruins under Thera's ash a "new Pompeii." His successors were learning that there had been a large town on the island; they were working along the south coast at its outer edges. Before the great eruption the town extended all the way across what was now the enormous caldera. From the southern to the northern tip of Thera's crescent was a distance of four miles. Some buildings had been sliced apart when the island's center collapsed. Ruins of their walls protruded from the face of the cliff more than a hundred feet above the bay.

One house northwest of Akrotiri had been literally cut in half. Its remaining rooms were at the brink of the cliff near Balos Bay. Two of them had served as storage quarters for grain. A pair of huge jars, a and d, were on opposite sides of room A. One contained carbonized barley, the other chopped straw. Smaller jars in room B held

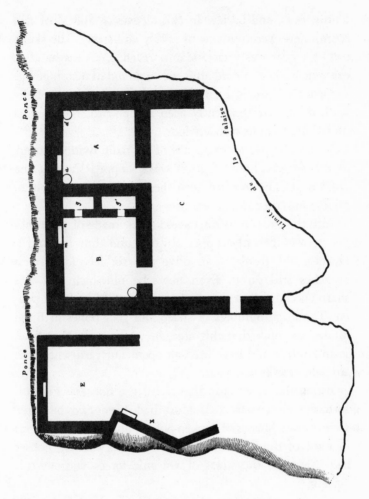

Plan of the Severed House, also by Mamet.
(Adapted from Fouqué, *Santorin et ses eruptions*).

lentils, peas, and barley. In two alcoves, g and g' of this room, there were remains of barley and straw. The skeleton of a goat was intact. Mamet reached out his hand to examine a piece of cord attached to the lid of a storage jar. It turned to dust in his fingers. A recessed portion of the wall, m–n, had apparently been a cupboard; they picked up fragments of its wooden door.

Room C appeared to be part of the main living quarters of this severed house, but its walls stopped short at the cliff's edge. The rest had been sheared off and gone plummeting into the caldera centuries ago.

In E the excavators discovered a saw made of pure copper. It was the only copper object found thus far, and it lay near the trunk of an olive tree six feet long, with branches still on it. Even now the nine-inch saw was sharp enough to cut deeply into soft wood like fir or poplar. The large numbers of sheep and goat bones in E led Mamet to think that this area, in which wall X was set at an angle, could have been an open courtyard where the animals were kept in pens.

Along the inner face of the cliff the houses were uniformly well constructed. Most had been two or three storeys high. Masses of broken pottery and buckled sections in some of the floors told a dramatic story: these houses had withstood the stress of volcanic forces without collapsing.

Mamet and Gorceix identified other animal bones, including those of rabbits, a donkey, and a dog and cat. Each site had its yield of household articles. Jars for storing foods were found filled with olives and with herbs such as anise and coriander. The kitchens of Theran women had well-stocked shelves. There were dozens of obsidian scrapers and knives. In several houses there were bathtubs and also mills to grind grain; weights for looms and fishing nets, and the tools used by carpenters. A gold ornament, a single black pottery bead, and a disk carved of the semi-precious stone serpentine were unusual little finds, the only ones that could be classified as jewelry. There was also evidence that the ancient Therans had a system of weights and measures that required the use of numerals and a balance.

When their work ended, the young Frenchmen could take satisfaction in realizing that they had made their own contribution to the new fund of knowledge about Thera's past. It was only four years ago, in 1866, that the crude walls on Therasia were first explored. By the time Mamet and Gorceix ended their brief campaign in 1870, a wealth of information had been gathered. It established beyond reasonable doubt that Thera's people were highly civilized. Because copper and gold had to be imported, the Therans must have relied on trade routes as the means for obtaining them. The town was a thriving community that needed the skills of potters, farmers, fishermen, masons, carpenters, weavers, and artists. Persons of rank and power could very well be the ones who enjoyed the touches of comfort and elegance in the larger houses.

But to some of the crucial questions about Thera there were no answers. The French could not assign a date to the devastating eruption. They could not determine the length of time afterward that "Most Beautiful Island" had been too barren and desolate to support human life. In short, no one really knew who these early Therans were or what became of them.

In 1874 Henri Mamet brought out a formal report of

his work with Gorceix. It was written as a thesis and in Latin, the language of scholars. This alone restricted the number of readers. In 1879 Ferdinand Fouqué published his own book, *Santorin et ses éruptions*. Although it was in French, it did not reach the reading public, nor was it intended to; essentially it was a geological study. Fouqué included a fascinating chapter about his own excavations and those of Mamet and Gorceix, but like the other, his book was known only to fellow-scientists. What is far more surprising is that these two studies failed to encourage others to continue the Thera excavations.

This may seem hard to believe today, when the world press gives generous coverage to archaeological discoveries. Why this apparent indifference?

It was a matter of timing. In 1873—three years after Mamet and Gorceix worked at Thera—a German named Heinrich Schliemann broke the dramatic news that he had found the ruins of ancient Troy. The whole world knew what Troy was, thanks to the writings of Homer. But who knew about Thera?

In 1873 Heinrich Schliemann was announcing the discovery of a ruined city he called the Troy of Homer. His excavation of a dusty hilltop site in Turkey had uncovered streets and dwellings protected by fortified walls, and a cache of golden jewelry. Everyone wanted to know more about this man and his work.

To the few who had heard about them at all, the buried houses on the volcanic island of Thera were dangerous and expensive to excavate; not even their discoverers seemed to know much about them. Schliemann and Troy overshadowed what the French had found.

It would be another century before Thera became important enough to compete for honors with Troy. In the life of the Atlantis legend, what was one century more or less?

XV

The Mystery of Ancient Crete

Those who wrote of their discoveries at Thera and Troy did not mention the legend of Atlantis. The journeys and books of John Lloyd Stephens had undermined its foothold in the Americas. He had demolished the idea that people from another land were the real builders of Maya cities. *Or had he?*

Instead of losing ground, the popularity of the legend was on the rise. Three men were composing their own variations on the Atlantis theme in these years. Brasseur and Le Plongeon were two of them, while the third was the volatile Ignatius Donnelly, Congressman from Minnesota. He was intently gathering the material for his book on Atlantis at the very same time that Fouqué, standing watch on Thera's volcano, found himself caught up in the problem of the buried houses.

When Donnelly's book appeared in 1882, he became the defender of the faith for all Atlantists. They ignored every historian who grumbled about his habit of mixing wishful fantasy with fact. Besides, the Atlantists could now point to Schliemann, who was not a trained scientist, as another hero. He was their shining example of a man who had proved the experts wrong. Troy had long been considered only a legend. Schliemann had shown that it actually existed. After his first campaign at Troy he went on to locate the shaft graves of Mycenae. There was treasure in them, a priceless collection of gold masks, jewels, and bowls of silver and gold. Schliemann had broken time's barriers. He had rediscovered the Mycenaeans, a Bronze Age people of the Greek mainland.

These soaring victories of faith over doubt and disbelief transformed the Atlantists' hopes into expectations. Religious mystics wove the legend into their spiritual teachings. It made its way into dozens of novels and stories. Atlantis would soon be found, the believers agreed, but no two groups could decide where. Some still rooted for Yucatán, some for the Azores or less familiar places. It was as if Stephens had never struggled and sweated through the jungles to track down the truth about the Maya.

Serious Atlantists kept up with reports of all archaeological excavations. A large number made after the 1880s had Greece as their focus. New methods of field work and technical analysis were developed by teams of men and women—French, Greek, British, American, German, almost too many to list. They worked sites with names known in history and the results were sometimes spectacular. Archaeology, one of the youngest sciences, was reaching full stature.

Even Thera had its share of attention. A little town of classical Greek times on Thera had priority for a German team, which excavated there in 1899. But Thera's buried ruins didn't interest them, even when one of the group scouted the Akrotiri region and uncovered a prehistoric lava house. In it Robert Zahn found timber fragments and jars containing carbonized food. The lid of one pottery jar had a strange sort of writing cut into its surface. A local farmer sold him a dagger blade that had turned up in his vineyard. Made of bronze inlaid with gold battle-axes, it was a superb weapon, worthy of a prince's hand.

But that ended the probe at Akrotiri. If Fouqué's work was remembered at all, the ash-smothered ruins so compellingly important to him were differently valued by the Germans. They concentrated on the classical site.

In the same year, 1899, Arthur Evans began excavating a six-acre complex of buildings at Knossos, on the island of Crete. Ancient tradition said it was the Palace of King Minos. Among these ruins, supposedly, was the Labyrinth where young Theseus of Athens slew the horrible Minotaur, a monster half human and half bull.

To Evans, King Minos was not legendary. He excavated the twisting maze of two- and three-storey buildings and found storerooms and shops where palace craftsmen had labored. At his own expense he began restoring warehouses for weapons; rooms used by officers of the palace guard; the private apartments of nobles; shrine rooms and broad ceremonial staircases. Tradition was justified. It was truly a palace, an intricate structure whose many buildings comprised one huge labyrinth.

Blade of a bronze dagger inlaid with gold axes, from Thera. Acquired by Robert Zahn in 1889. (Courtesy of National Museum, Copenhagen, Denmark.)

Schliemann had followed Homer's words as his guide in hunting for Troy. Impressed by this, Evans kept in mind the saying of Homer that Crete had a hundred towns. This British archaeologist, like Schliemann, was an amateur. His work drew criticism. It proved beyond question, however, that the people he named the Minoans in honor of King Minos were highly advanced in statecraft and the arts. They ruled a strong but peaceable empire, and by 1600 B.C. their control of the eastern Mediterranean region was absolute. Their fleet of fast, reliable merchant ships, some with thirty oars on either side, served as the first line of defense. These kept open the trade routes and carried Minoan goods, spreading their economic influence to Egypt, Syria, and as far to the west as Sicily.

The excavations dramatically changed the picture of early life in the Aegean area. That murky period of time so vaguely called "prehistory" was illumined first at Mycenae and then by the revelations at Knossos. For history and archaeology they were a tremendous breakthrough.

What Arthur Evans discovered was another unknown civilization. The Minoans emerged from the forgotten past as a highly creative people whose culture was older than that of the Mycenaeans. Like patient workers sorting and assembling bits of plaster to restore a fresco, archaeologists could see the patterns of another Bronze Age society take form.

The objects recovered at Knossos were beyond price. In making beautiful pottery and in gem and ivory carving the Minoans had no peers. Their skill in working metals, especially bronze and gold, was matchless. Frescoes on the ruined palace walls showed both men and women elegantly dressed, wearing jewelry as unique as their hair styles. In other frescoes young men and women acrobats played a daring game of leaping over bulls while spectators watched in the central courtyard.

They were, these Minoans, just about as sophisticated in their tastes as any people of the modern world. They enjoyed music, dancing, and the sports of boxing and javelin throwing. The men were skilled archers. Luxury was the keynote of palace life: its bathrooms had running water and drainage systems.

All these discoveries stemmed from Evans' early years of work. But a mystery had surfaced. Inside the palace he found signs of heavy damage by fire. Burned-out sections in some buildings indicated that violent fires had struck several times during its long history.

After the first one, which he thought had occurred between 1800 and 1700 B.C., the Palace of Minos was completely redesigned and rebuilt. A bold new style of art and architecture was introduced. Minoan culture came to full flowering at this time. Evans placed it at 1600 B.C.

Fire attacked the palace again about a century and a half after the rebuilding. The element of mystery was the relationship of these fires to the sudden downfall of the Minoans. Just when it seemed invincibly secure, their empire began to weaken. A generation before the last fire it was in sharp decline. After it, in no more than fifty years, the empire collapsed. The Minoans themselves, once the proud lords of the seaways, simply disappeared.

As the man who had discovered their very existence, Evans was baffled. Something had happened that stripped the rulers of their power, and it happened *before* the last fire. He dated that final fire at approximately 1450 B.C. By 1400, he estimated from studying the evidence, the palace was abandoned.

Crete was fertile soil for archaeology. The work at Knossos was in its initial stages when the site of another Minoan palace was discovered, then others. *Their excavators found that most of them, including their nearby farms and towns, had been leveled by fire at one and the same time.* They had been deserted immediately. A few were reoccupied, but only after an interval and then briefly. Knossos was the exception. Although it was again damaged by flames, it did not burn to the ground. Some rebuilding was done. People stayed on. They lived like squatters, meanly and with few comforts.

The vexing question for archaeologists was this: Were the great fires a man-made holocaust or the result of a natural happening? That is, did an invading army relentlessly put the torch to all the palaces and villas, or was it a disastrous blow of nature, such as an earthquake, that brought about their fiery end? In either case, why was Knossos spared? From all the evidence, Knossos was the administrative center of Crete where its priest-king lived. It went on functioning after other palaces were abandoned. What seemed at first to be only a coincidence became a major historical mystery.

By 1911 Evans had received many honors. His government conferred a knighthood on him. But his critics were now more outspoken. They disputed his methods of reconstructing Knossos. Since he owned the site, he had full authority over it. Fellow scientists were not permitted to see the hoards of clay tablets he had recovered; their study might clarify the problem.

Evans was a law unto himself. He ignored criticism. One view that opposed his own held that Knossos could have been captured by invaders before the last fire, perhaps by the mainland Mycenaeans. But Evans disagreed. He looked on Mycenae as a colony of Minoan Crete. He called its culture "inferior" and would not consider the possibility that the Minoans were early Greeks. Other archaeologists thought they could have been.

The clash of personalities and opinions was pushed aside by a series of alarming political moves in the Balkans. In 1912 Greece reclaimed Crete from the Turks, who had held it for five centuries. Next, she declared war on Turkey. For anxious months the peace of Europe was threatened. Using his influence as a friend of both nations, Evans was trying to mediate when England declared war on Germany in 1914.

Work stopped at sites throughout Europe and the Near East. Knossos was deserted once more. Weeds grew back among its freshly excavated ruins.

A few months before the outbreak of war a new and entirely original theory about Minoan Crete appeared in a British archaeological journal. There could not have been a worse time for its publication. In this moment of international tension it was overlooked by those who were closest to the problem of ancient Crete. Many of them were now involved in the war. That fact alone may be why the theory went unnoticed.

But it, too, was a discovery, made not on the site of an actual excavation but in the realm of thought. The young man who presented it had found a strong resemblance between Minoan Crete and the Atlantis of Plato. He saw certain parallels between the two that could not be explained by chance or coincidence.

Plato's story of Atlantis, he said, is believable if it is looked at through the eyes of the ancient Egyptians. They knew about the downfall of a distant kingdom. Its disappearance must have seemed to them as abrupt and tragic *as if the sea had opened to swallow it.*

For the first time archaeology was called on to interpret the story of Atlantis and its destruction as Plato told it.

Crete—and *Atlantis!*

It was another breakthrough.

XVI

A Vision of Atlantis

The man who saw a likeness to doomed Atlantis in Crete's ruined palaces was K. T. Frost. He was not an archaeologist, but he had an archaeologist's grasp of the problem revealed by the recent excavations. Professor Frost was a classical scholar on the faculty of Queen's University, Belfast.

The London *Times* published his first outline of the theory. "Knossos and its allied cities were swept away just when they seemed strongest and safest," he said as early as 1909. "It was as if the whole kingdom had sunk in the sea, as if the tale of Atlantis were true . . . The whole description of Atlantis which is given in the *Timaeus* and the *Critias* (Plato's writings) has features so thoroughly Minoan that even Plato could not have invented so many unsuspected facts."

In a 1913 article prepared for a scholarly journal, Frost gave the reasons he had for accepting much of the Atlantis story as perfectly sound history. First of all, there is good evidence that Solon was in Egypt about 591 B.C. and while he was there it would have been strange if he had *not* called on the priests of Saïs; their reputation for wisdom fascinated the Greeks.

At the start, then, Frost was breaking with the strong tradition that everything in Plato's story was imaginary. His approach was to review it as Plato told it and to analyze the contents *from the Egyptian point of view.* This makes possible a completely new interpretation. Many of Plato's descriptions seem contradictory. Some appear to border on fantasy. But with the change in perspective that Frost suggests, they make good sense.

If Solon visited Saïs, as Frost thought he did, then it would have been natural for a priest to tell him about a great but generally forgotten event out of the past. The part played by the Athenians in the story was a compliment to his Greek guest. Also, simply by telling it, the priest was illustrating the fact that the Egyptians had historical records no other nations possessed.

"Solon was a poet no less than a politician," Frost wrote, "and it was by a political poem which still survives that he first won fame." In the priest's story he must have seen the elements of a stirring epic poem. When the powerful empire turned from peace to war and attacked friendly nations, the gods were angered. Zeus commanded the sea to overwhelm it. "The story as it stands sounds like an impossible romance," Frost conceded. "If however we are content to say that the island empire and not the island itself was destroyed suddenly and finally, then an exact parallel did actually occur."

Instead of looking at the ancient story as the work of Plato's creative genius, Frost made a forceful case for it as a series of plausible happenings. He was much amused by the popular idea that a vast island in the Atlantic Ocean was ". . . once the seat of a great civilisation when the rest of the world was more or less barbarous, and that from it other civilisations have sprung; but that it suddenly sank in the sea." (Was he poking fun at Donnelly and his fans?) He argued that it was futile to look for Atlantis as a submerged continent. "On the other hand, a political and national disaster . . . can destroy an ancient civilisation as completely as any flood, and on these lines it may be possible to find the central historic fact which gave rise to the legend."

He drew on the writings of ancient and modern historians to explain what the Egyptians of the Bronze Age knew about Minoan Crete. Very little, Frost said flatly. They were vague about its location. Egyptian ships did not venture far, if at all, into the waters Crete controlled. It was a faraway and mysterious empire dominating the "Great Green Sea," as they called the Mediterranean. Their name for Crete was Keftiu and its people were Keftians. It was located *before the Pillars of Hercules,* they knew; they were aware that another body of water was farther west than that, *beyond the Pillars.* More than this they did not know.

Frost now put his finger on one of the most baffling of Plato's descriptions: his statement that the island empire lay "beyond" or "outside" the Pillars of Hercules and in the Atlantic Ocean. The very name *Atlantis* has added

to the confusion. But as Frost observed, "To anyone sailing from Egypt, Crete is in front of the Pillars and the
Atlantic is behind them." With the changed point of view,
Plato's words accurately describe Crete. The most diligent
Atlantis seekers have looked in the wrong direction because they took Plato literally. He was only repeating the
description Solon took from the Egyptians!

As to the history contained in the Egyptian story Frost
detected two separate events. The first was the downfall
of Minoan Crete. The Egyptians had to realize that tragedy had struck Crete when its ships suddenly disappeared.
After centuries of friendly trade the Keftians seemed to
vanish *as if their empire had sunk in the sea.*

Frost offered his own explanation of the cause: Crete's
wealthy palaces fell in an attack by raiding parties who
poured in from Greece. He used the date Evans had
worked out for the fall of Knossos as the time when all
the palaces were sacked and burned, about 1400 B.C.
They were rich and vulnerable. The Minoans relied on
ships to protect their island. A sneak attack, Frost thought,
was their undoing. Under the leadership of Mycenae,
power shifted to the invaders.

The Mycenaeans became the new masters of the island-
empire. Instead of destroying Minoan culture, they spread
it more widely than before. But its days of greatness were
past. In his words, "Its creative force was spent." The
work of its artists and builders soon lost its excellence.
Under Mycenaean rule Crete of the Minoans began to die.

The second event Frost saw in the Egyptian story was a
clash between armies two centuries after the invasion.
Rameses III was Pharoah of Egypt. Allies from Asia
Minor joined the aggressive Mycenaeans in what Frost

described as "a mighty confederacy, formed as it was of the rovers of the sea, of the pirate princes, and fierce warriors who live in the lines of Homer." They launched a massive drive on Egypt by land and sea.

Pharoah's armies confronted them somewhere on the coast of Palestine or the Nile Delta. In 1194 B.C. they were defeated. The stunning Egyptian triumph went into the priestly records as a victory over the rulers of the Great Green Sea. To the Egyptians, who were unaware of the revolutionary changes in Crete, there seemed no difference between the Minoans and their successors, the Mycenaeans.

Frost was convinced that the tale Solon heard in Egypt was a garbled account of the two events. He went on to point out the many parallels that make Plato's Atlantis seem almost a mirror image of Minoan Crete. An impressive list of them closes the article. Reading his words, one catches something of his extraordinary vision. He looked behind the legend and found the substance of reality.

Speaking of Plato's idealized kingdom of Atlantis, he said, "The great harbour with its shipping and its merchants coming from all parts is typical of Crete: the elaborate bathrooms . . . are striking features of the Minoan scheme of life, and the solemn sacrifice of a bull was a Minoan ceremony. It is true that these points of resemblance are not in themselves enough to prove Minoan origin, but this inference is warranted when we read that 'the bull is hunted in the Temple of Poseidon without weapons but with staves and nooses.' This cannot be anything but a description of the Bull-ring at Cnossus, the very thing which struck foreigners most . . . and gave rise to the legend of the Minotaur . . . This bullfight as

we know from frescoes in the palace of Cnossus itself
. . . differed from all others in the very point that Plato
emphasises, namely that no weapons were used.

"It is not impossible therefore that Solon went to Egypt
and learned what was in fact the Egyptian version of the
overthrow of the Minoans, although he did not recognize
it as such; that he used it as the basis of the epic which
he never completed, but the plot of which Plato knew and
adapted to his own use. This view is at least consistent
with known facts."

If Professor Frost hoped that his theory would be given
serious attention, he was disappointed. If he had plans for
future research, World War I canceled them. He was
killed in action. Although his article was ignored at the
time, it is credited today with setting new guidelines for
the study of materials that were the source of Plato's
Atlantis story.

In 1932 a young Greek archaeologist, Spyridon Marinatos, was working near Knossos. Discoveries he made
there turned his thoughts away from Crete and toward the
crescent-shaped island of Thera, sixty miles north. He
knew its history of violent eruptions, and he had read
Ferdinand Fouqué's important book. Slowly, cautiously,
Marinatos developed a theory of his own about the reason
for Crete's downfall. It was more complete than the theories of Evans and Frost. Unlike Frost, whose work he admired, Marinatos had the archaeologist's approach to
problems of interpreting the past. Amnisos, an ancient
town near Knossos, provided the clue, the missing key to
the puzzle, that neither Evans nor Frost had reckoned

with. Marinatos finally put his theory to the test by excavating on the island of Thera.

By 1967 his name, his discoveries, and the Atlantis
legend were headline news the world around.

XVII

Written in the Earth

Thirty-five centuries ago Amnisos, on the north coast of Crete, was the harbor town of Knossos. Marinatos was excavating two Minoan houses there in 1932. One of them stood on a small hill overlooking the sparkling-clear water. It was named "Villa of the Frescoes" after a wall painting of lilies and other flowers was found in one room.

At first Marinatos was puzzled by something quite strange about this ancient house, and he couldn't dismiss it from his mind. He brought a searching, inquiring attitude to his work. The smallest detail did not escape notice. On one occasion he said that the archaeologist deciphers "a special language," which he defined as "the language that the centuries have written into the earth. But it is a language you can only read once: while you are digging."

At nineteen he had become junior director of the archaeological museum of Crete. Ten years later he was its director. He was thirty-one the year he excavated at Amnisos, and he held degrees earned in Germany and at the University of Athens. He was fast becoming a seasoned campaigner in field archaeology. To this demanding work, which he loved, Marinatos brought a rare combination of talent, enthusiasm, and insight.

What struck him as peculiar about the Villa of Lilies was the odd way its outer walls were tilted. They consisted of huge, well-cut limestone blocks. All but two were in place, but some tremendous force had pried them from an upright position and made them bulge outwards. The inner walls and corners of rooms had fallen in. Marks of scorching fire were everywhere.

His first thought was that the heavy walls had been wrenched out of position by a tidal wave. Such a wave, or *tsunami,* as Japanese scientists have named it, is produced by an underwater earthquake or volcanic eruption. It travels at high speed and after striking the coast, floods inland. The damage done by the first shock is intensified when the receding water exerts power enough to tow tons of rubble back with it.

The missing blocks and the tilt of the others in the Villa could be explained by wave action, but the fire was a different matter. Wood was used extensively in Minoan architecture. Clearly it was used here though none remained. Even the stone bases that once supported wooden pillars were blackened. "This was a great problem," Marinatos wrote later, "as I could not reconcile the fire with a terrible inundation caused by the sea." And he could not forget it.

He made a second discovery in the other Minoan house, closer to the water. Its basement was filled with masses of sand and pumice stone. In the corner of one room Marinatos came upon a square pit completely filled with pumice. Each piece was rounded and polished like a pebble.

In small amounts, pumice is often found along the shores of Greek islands. Pieces constantly tumble into the sea from Thera and are light enough to drift hundreds of miles. Nothing like this large deposit had ever been found in Crete. In his first report on the 1932 excavations, he made a frank guess: the pumice could have been gathered and stored by a Minoan trader who intended to barter with it. Pumice is simply one form of volcanic glass. Then, as now, it is used as a cleaning and polishing agent because it is easily ground into powder.

When the real explanation for both findings occurred to him, Marinatos had to consider all that was known about the prehistoric eruption that destroyed Thera and then take a long, hard look at how much was still unknown. The oddly canted walls of the villa signaled to him that during the eruption there had been one or several tsunami. And the scorch marks? Fires must have started when little household oil lamps toppled over in buildings smashed by waves from Thera. The pit filled with pumice was not a trader's hoard at all but an accidental buildup of wave-borne material. Commenting years later, Marinatos said that one could reconstruct what had happened:

"When the waves broke the building was carried away almost to its foundations. Then it lay abandoned and after a time the north breezes brought the pumice stone from the volcano as far as Crete. As this building stands on the shore, it was constantly inundated by the sea and the rooms were thus covered with pumice stone."

There was only one explanation for the finding. It was

not warfare, not a terrible earthquake, but volcanic action.
If Thera had the potential for destruction that he now
suspected, other evidence had to exist.

In mountain areas and on the plains of Crete, and
eventually on Thera, Marinatos had his suspicions confirmed. He gradually deciphered the language written by
the centuries into the earth. The clues and signs he found
between 1932 and 1939 pointed straight to Thera, sixty
miles north of Amnisos.

The eruption had several phases. He was sure of that,
though not of their timing or sequence. Each one did
incalculable damage. Together, they disrupted life on
Minoan Crete. He was beginning to see a chain reaction
of volcanic disturbances that included earthshocks and
tsunami of prodigious size. The volcano had spewed out
poisonous fumes along with intermittent showers of fiery
ash and molten pumice.

It was evident to him that each stage was manifested
differently in various regions of Crete. How any one region was affected depended on its distance from Thera and
from the coast, and also on the geological structure of the
earth under it. When Thera blew apart, its center and
some of its west coast plunged into the sea. Water rushed
into the boiling void, then rebounded in the form of
towering waves. Spreading out, they smashed coastal settlements hundreds of miles distant. What he observed at
Amnisos told Marinatos that Crete had been relentlessly
battered by huge waves.

Why had the eruption been ignored as the cause of
the Minoan downfall? During the years of excavation
and discovery in Crete, archaeologists had been reporting
what they found at one or another of the many sites. Like

the blind men and the elephant of the fable, each reported accurately on a segment of the whole. Marinatos knew from experience that archaeologists seldom study much volcanology. Eruptions were the business of geologists and volcanologists. No one had tried to assess the effects of Thera's eruption. No one had suggested that it could have made Crete unlivable.

Evans had not. In 1926 Sir Arthur lived through a severe earthquake at Knossos. This unnerving experience convinced him that an earthquake was the destroyer of life and wrecker of Minoan cities. A deep rumble like the sound of a roaring bull sometimes precedes a major upheaval of the earth. Evans had heard it. "It is something," he wrote, "to have heard with one's own ears the bellowing of the bull beneath the earth, who, according to primitive belief, tosses it with its horns." In worshipping their Mother Earth goddess, he said, the Minoans were appealing to her for protection from that raging beast of the underworld. And as poignant testimony of their dread he offered the countless statues and frescoes of bulls he had found at Knossos.

Frost had not reckoned with the eruption. Unlike the "dirt archaeologists," however, his purpose was to identify Minoan Crete with Atlantis. He blamed the Minoan downfall on invading Mycenaeans, who he said seized their palaces with torch and sword. And he let it go at that.

Though no one else did, Marinatos remembered that Ferdinand Fouqué and his two colleagues had explored buried houses on Thera whose walls were intact to heights of six and seven feet. On the other hand, the ruins of some Cretan buildings had the rippled floors and jagged cracks that are the signature of earthquakes, while others did not. Marinatos found it impossible to assume, as Evans did, that all these were simultaneously destroyed in the course of a single earthquake—leaving only Knossos to survive a few years longer.

By 1939 he was confident enough of his work to publish its results in *Antiquity,* a British archaeological journal. "The Volcanic Destruction of Minoan Crete" he called the article. Those six words heralded a precedent-shattering theory. He reconstructed a natural disaster greater in magnitude than any other in human history.

For the approximate date of the eruption he used 1500 B.C. It accorded remarkably well with the time period worked out by Evans for the mysterious decline of Minoan power. *It also was the date archaeologists now assigned to the types of pottery found on Thera by Gorceix and Mamet seventy years earlier.*

A distinctive quality about the article—and this is aside from its scientific contribution—is that it puts meaning into the words "a natural disaster." Marinatos considers the feelings and emotions of the terrified, bewildered people who were caught in the tragedy. Forces they could not comprehend become immediate and real as he recreates the horrors of their days and nights when the sea turned wild, fire and mud rained down from the darkened sky, and the earth trembled under their feet.

XVIII

Not by Conquering Armies

Volcanoes, like people, belong to families. Marinatos used this geological fact to reconstruct the ancient eruption by comparing it with one that shocked the world in 1883. Krakatoa, a tiny volcanic island in Indonesia, blew apart that year with a roar heard two thousand miles away. Eyewitness reports and follow-up studies by scientists tell its awesome story.

Thera and Krakatoa are classified as volcanoes of the same type. In historic times their eruptions have been similar: violent and explosive, releasing deadly gases and blowing fragmented materials high in the air. Italy's Mount Vesuvius and Mount Saint Helens in Washington are in this group. They are sometimes referred to as the Plinian type, after the Roman naturalist Pliny who died in 79 A.D. when Pompeii was destroyed by Mount Vesuvius's eruption.

Another type includes volcanoes that cause lava flows but are rarely explosive. Still a third "family" combines characteristics of the other two, but the distinctions are not clear-cut.

For the purpose of showing what could have happened at Thera, Marinatos relied on the recorded events of the Krakatoa disaster. The account of them is, in his words, "truly amazing."

The island of Krakatoa is located in the Sunda Strait, the narrow channel between Java and Sumatra where the Indian Ocean joins the Sea of Java. Its long-dormant volcano became active in May, 1883, when a column of dust and vapor spurted into the air and showers of pumice fell. Since earthquakes were very minor and only one of Krakatoa's three volcanic cones was active, no one was seriously alarmed. Then, too, the little island was not inhabited.

The crisis came in August. On Sunday, the 26th of that month, there were frequent loud, explosive booms. All three cones were erupting, making the air vibrate with their thunderous noise. Sound and shock waves broke windows and damaged the walls of houses a hundred miles from Krakatoa. The outfall of ash became thick enough to fill the sky. Daylight turned to darkness.

People in western Java were kept awake all night by the roars and flashes from the volcano. Any objects in or near their homes that were free and loose were moved about, not because of earthquakes—these were barely noticeable—but by the vibrating atmosphere. Marinatos described that night: ". . . crashes, bangs, clashes, creakings and crashings resounded everywhere, causing physical and mental agony. The crashes were followed by complete silence, which was equally terrifying and caused widespread nervous hysteria."

By early morning the sounds resumed, more deafening than before. After ten o'clock it grew dark again as a cloud of yellowish-gray smoke poured from Krakatoa and cold mists rained down. Lamps fell from their supports, windows and doors were thrown open in far distant buildings. The air was tinged with a slight smell of sulphuric acid. Too frightened to leave their owners, domestic animals refused to go away from them and the light of their lamps even when dragged.

Ash fell a thousand miles from the volcano. Fine particles rose into the stratosphere, where they were picked up by air currents and dispersed over the entire earth, thirty miles above its surface. For months afterward the brilliant sunsets were blazing reminders of Krakatoa.

While the eruption was at its peak on Monday, the island and the Indian Ocean for miles about were littered with vast quantities of floating pumice. To add to the horror, winds of gale force suddenly sprang up. In the already electrified atmosphere, lightning struck people and tall buildings. Burning ash hot enough to blister and kill dropped over wide areas.

The heaviest explosions came each time one of Krakatoa's volcanic cones collapsed. When the last one collapsed, two-thirds of the island's center ripped apart, then plunged into the sea. The sound of that explosion was the greatest of all. A basin-shaped caldera was formed that is like Thera's but only one-fourth as large. All this while, huge chunks of pumice and soil were being flung fifty miles from the island.

When the center of the island submerged, the ocean

was violently agitated by the shift of such volumes of water. It churned into the smoldering cavity and rebounded as towering tsunami. They were ninety feet high, moved incredibly fast, and smashed against the coasts of Sumatra and Java. Even after striking the coasts they were still forty-five feet high as they rushed half a mile inland.

"Whole towns, villages, and woods were destroyed," Marinatos wrote, "and great masses of stones from the sea were hurled far inland." Trains and boats were later found scattered about on high ground. One large ship had been carried more than a mile inland from a bay in Sumatra.

The houses of one coastal town in Java were set on fire three different times in the space of two hours. Each wave tore them from their foundations. Lamps overturned, starting fires inside the houses. With each returning wave they were extinguished, then rekindled by the intensely hot volcanic material. Altogether there were three tsunami.

Because Marinatos remembered the reports he had read of this particular episode, it had been his first and all-important clue to the meaning of the Amnisos discoveries. He drew this parallel: "We can, then, suppose that by the time the waves from Thera reached Crete it was night, or the day had been transformed into night and the inhabitants had lit the lamps. . . ." It was a graphic explanation of the signs of fire he had detected in the waterfront buildings of Amnisos.

The tsunami and floods of 1883 killed 36,000 people. In magnitude and intensity, however, the eruption of Thera was enormously greater. The anguish felt by the people of Sumatra and Java is a matter of record. What the anguished Minoans of Crete felt cannot be imagined.

Dr. Spyridon Marinatos. (Photograph by Spiros Meletzis.)

They could not have understood the reason for the ear-splitting noises or the darkness that blotted out the sun. They could only think that their mother goddess had turned on them in fury. The tremendous vibration of the air assuredly caused extensive damage, making roofs fall in, literally shaking houses to pieces. "Then must have come the rain of mud and ashes, some cold, some ablaze and burning."

In the case of Krakatoa, the worst destruction was done by tidal floods. Marinatos estimated that the tsunami were higher and moved more swiftly in the Aegean Sea. Thera lost thirty-two square miles when its crater caved in, compared with Krakatoa, which lost eight square miles. Between Thera and Crete the sea is much deeper than the Indian Ocean near the Sunda Strait. The deeper the water over which a flood wave moves, the faster it travels. In every respect, Thera has to be considered the more devastating of the two disasters. There is no means of estimating the lives lost on Thera. Unlike Krakatoa it was well populated. There is no way to guess the death toll there or in Crete and other islands, in Asia Minor, and probably as far away as Egypt.

Amnisos was only one of the coastal towns to be destroyed. Depending on the height of the flood waters, many towns in the coastal plains were also wiped out. Marinatos described a site where excavators in 1922 found huge double axes, sacred objects used in religious ceremonies. They lay on the floor of the room where they had been dropped. At another site a carpenter's shop and a coppersmith's were found intact. People had no warning of oncoming floods. He wrote, "I think there is little reason to doubt that the devastation of the coast sites . . . was caused by the waves from the eruption of Thera." Those waves took barely half an hour to reach Crete.

That left still unexplained the condition of the ruined palaces on higher ground. Because of their elevation they had been secure from floods. Marinatos suggested that they were demolished by earthquakes. Before and after the eruption of Krakatoa, he wrote, exceptionally heavy quakes shook nearby areas. In the case of Crete they might have come before the eruption but more probably afterward. During the years that Thera's activity has been recorded, earthquakes have always occurred before and after eruptions, never at the same time. It seemed to him that this would be equally true of prehistoric Thera. He reminded his readers that ancient buildings found buried under ash and pumice on the island had walls with no earthquake scars whatever. Shocks that came after the eruption did not disturb them; they were insulated against them. But he argued that earthquakes would account for the destruction of inland villas and palaces. Unaffected by the floods, they were later brought to ruin by earthquakes.

With clear-cut examples like these, Marinatos offered plausible scientific solutions to some of the most imposing problems archaeologists had encountered in Crete for the past thirty years. In recreating the drama of this event he never lost sight of the human condition. Many Minoans, he thought, became refugees. He mentioned the Keftiu shown in Egyptian frescoes and wondered whether they might have been survivors who had fled Crete to settle in northern Syria. Farmers whose land was blanketed with pumice and ash could not work the soil for an unknown length of time. The fishing villages of the coast were gone, and with them vitally important supplies of food from the sea.

Crete had been dealt an irreparable blow. Its system of orderly government was in disarray. Its merchant ships had been battered and sunk in their wrecked harbors. The island was undefended. Whatever power remained was centered at Knossos.

After 1400 even Knossos was abandoned and simultaneously, he wrote, the first wave of invaders descended. These were the Mycenaeans, who were beginning to expand and reach out for colonies. Crete was within their grasp. Marinatos warned that one need not imagine a violent conquest. It was less a matter of their seizing control than of taking over without resistance now that Crete was vulnerable for the first time in hundreds of years.

Not all the customs and products of an advanced culture had vanished. The newcomers found many of them to their liking and adapted them to their own use. For instance, the Cretans had developed archery into a science. It was a welcome addition to the invaders' weaponry. As they built up their own trade routes, Crete's new masters needed the products of artists and craftsmen. But as archaeology had already shown, these products soon lost their distinctive Minoan character.

"A civilization of 2000 years' standing does not disappear without leaving a trace," said Marinatos. Minoan laws and religion had lasting influences as the Mycenaean way of life merged with the Minoan. Old traditions were durable enough to leave their mark on the Dorians, the people who later came as invaders to challenge Mycenaean rule and eventually to succeed them. By 1000 B.C. the Mycenaean civilization in its turn had ceased to exist.

Marinatos was the first scientist of the twentieth century to look so intently at prehistoric Thera in order to search out the effects of its eruption on Crete. His decision was that it acted as the trigger mechanism for floods and fires and for earthquakes. This was the catastrophe that brought the Minoans to their knees, not conquering armies.

His article was published the same year that Marinatos became professor of archaeology at the University of Athens. Every page of it reveals his long experience in field excavation and research.

The response to it is still difficult to explain. Several archaeologists who had worked in Crete replied that they had found no evidence of flooding on their sites, let alone any traces of volcanic pumice or ash. Others were critical; it was, they said, "too sensational."

Like the earlier work by K. T. Frost, the theory appeared as Europe was mobilizing for another great war. Only two months before its publication, England and France declared war on Germany, which had invaded Poland. Tanks, planes, and troops were on the move.

During World War II precious little archaeological research or digging went on in Crete. Nazi soldiers occupied the island.

Not surprisingly, in 1950 Marinatos carried his theory one step further. In another article, hardly noticed at the time because it appeared only in the Greek language, he said that Plato's story had been inspired by the destruction of Thera, "beyond all measure, powerful and rich." Dimly remembered but muddled accounts of ancient wars and disasters had their origin in the Bronze Age eruption. Marinatos would never retreat from that position. With equal fervor he believed that the eruption caused the abandonment of Crete's palaces.

Any chance of leading an excavation that would test these theories of his didn't seem remotely possible at the time. It was too expensive. The work would be as difficult as it would be dangerous.

Strangely enough, an earthquake in the Aegean Sea drew one more scientist into the search for links between Atlantis and Thera. This man, like Ferdinand Fouqué, was enthralled by an accidental glimpse of what lay hidden in the pumice mine. Since no one could explain what he had seen, he promptly set out to find the answer for himself.

XIX

The Undetected Error

🌿 Forty-eight persons were killed and many others injured when an earthquake shook Thera in 1956. Half the houses in the villages crumbled apart. An early arrival at the stricken island was Professor Angelos Galanopoulos. He was director of the Athens Seismological Institute, and he came to inspect the damage.

In the course of his official duties he learned that the heavy quake had uncovered some prehistoric objects in the pumice mine near Phirá. Its owner took him to the lowest level. What Galanopoulos beheld down there made a profound impression on his thinking.

The walls of a stone house stood upright a hundred feet below the surface. In one wall he could see pottery fragments and stone tools. Inside the house he was able to gather up a few human bones and teeth, two of them badly burnt; some olive leaves; some pieces of charred wood.

Could anyone forget such an experience? His tours of inspection made Galanopoulos a daily witness to Thera's suffering. The same restless forces, which eons ago buried the stone house under hot ash, were still ominously active. Like Marinatos at Amnisos, he suddenly realized how very little was known about the consequences of the great eruption. Even its date was uncertain. To this man, whose sphere of concern was earthquakes and tsunami, an intensive study of the ancient disaster seemed long overdue.

He sent the teeth and the wood to the Lamont Geological Laboratory of New York for radiocarbon testing. This was a new method of measuring the age of rocks and organic materials. Like humans, living animals and plants constantly absorb radiocarbon from the atmosphere. A sample of aged bone or wood is tested for the amount of radiocarbon it retains; it gives this off in the form of radioactivity. Analysis can often determine the age of the sample—the approximate date of its death—with considerable accuracy.

He was notified that the teeth were those of a man in his thirties and a woman in her forties. They died not earlier than 1510 nor later than 1310 B.C. The objective report was very close to the date Marinatos had first proposed for the eruption: 1500 B.C.

The discovery of those pitiful human remains was the accident that started Professor Galanopoulos on his own investigation of Thera's past. In 1960, he was invited to address an international conference of earth scientists in Helsinki, Finland. His subject was the tsunami of ancient times. Only a few friends knew that he was about to offer a solution to what he called "the Atlantis riddle."

Some details were still to be worked out, he explained. Even so, the theory he outlined to that gathering of scientists immediately put Atlantis into the newspapers of the world, usually as a page one item. It may turn out to be as close as any theory can ever come to solving the riddle.

His presentation was extraordinary. Everything the twentieth century has learned about the Minoans has inspired new interpretations of Plato's story. But Galanopoulos had tapped fresh sources of information from the geophysical sciences as well as archaeology. Crucial as these were, he had also discovered an error in the text of Plato's tale that has gone completely undetected. And in this he saw an important clue to the identity of Atlantis.

Many who heard his initial discussion encouraged him to continue his research and seek to clear up the remaining problems. This he did. Four months later Galanopoulos announced that the solution to the riddle was complete in all respects.

It was the effects of the Thera eruption that first made him question their bearing on Plato's story. The tsunami and floods that followed the collapse of the crater were more destructive than any in recorded history. He was convinced that they explain the tale of an island-continent "swallowed by the sea." And he thought they lie behind the old myth about Deucalion, a Noah-like figure who rode out a worldwide deluge in a little boat with his wife. They were the sole survivors when Zeus angrily drowned the rest of humanity for its wickedness.

His search for a connection between the Atlantis story and the Bronze Age eruption was fruitful. He found not one but a number of links. He had studied every report written about the occurrence of seismic waves from ancient times to the present. The Atlantis story itself he now believed to be history—distorted and blurred, but history nonetheless. Dim memories of the calamity were the story's source and substance.

It was a strong stand to take, but he was sure of his ground because of that curious error in Plato's tale, which he had discovered. It is this: In the Greek text, whenever Plato uses dates or gives dimensions *in the thousands,* they are ten times too large. The dimensions of the fertile plain make it too big to have been anywhere in the Mediterranean Sea. Plato says it measured 230 by 345 miles, or 79,350 square miles.

But what happens when the first two figures are divided by ten? They become 23 miles by 34.5! An island of that size would easily fit within the limits of the Mediterranean Sea and even inside its eastern arm, the Aegean Sea.

Historians have good reason to smile at the figure 9,000. According to Plato, it was that many years after Atlantis sank that Solon went to Egypt. Again, when 9,000 is reduced by a factor of ten, it becomes 900. Now, it is not a tradition but a historic fact that Solon was in Egypt about 580 B.C., *almost exactly 900 years after Thera exploded.* One correction cancels a tenfold error in the size of Atlantis. The other cancels an error in time.

Could this be only a coincidence? Galanopoulos thought not, because it is absolutely consistent. He suggested that it was made either by the priest who told the story to Solon, or by Solon himself, and it happened when the Egyptian language was being translated into Greek. The Egyptian word or symbol for the number 100 was confused with the symbol for 1,000.

Solon made notes on the story just as the priest told it,

complete with numbers and dates. While he did not use it to write an epic poem as he hoped, the manuscript after his death was entrusted to members of his family and was still in their possession at the time Plato lived. Galanopoulos accepted this as a logical statement of fact. If it were not true, numbers and dimensions would not be included in Plato's story in such detail. In order to be so consistent they had to be preserved in written form.

The tenfold error inflates the number of land allotments and the quotas of military equipment and fighting men required for the defense of Atlantis. It exaggerates the length of the canal around the plain and the distances of its cross trenches. In speaking of the plain, Plato's tale says that the size of its man-made canal does seem "incredible."

One set of figures is not affected by the tenfold error. Whenever Plato gives numbers in units of tens of stades, they seem to be accurate. In the Greek text the dimensions of the Metropolis are in units of stades. None of them is more than a hundred. They can be taken at face value.

To demonstrate how his discovery relates Thera to Atlantis, Galanopoulos used two maps when he addressed the conference. One was based on a British Admiralty chart and showed Thera as it is today, a broken cluster of small islands. Over this he placed the second map. It was a design of the Metropolis and outer city of Atlantis drawn to scale according to Plato's own measurements in stades.

The fit was very close. The ancient acropolis fitted neatly into the center of the caldera where only the Kameni islands are now. The Metropolis with its land and water rings, up to and including the outer city wall, was contained within the perimeter of the Thera group. It was at once dramatically clear that in preeruption days Thera was large enough and appropriately shaped to be the site of Plato's fabulous city.

Galanopoulos also made use of a chart adapted from a modern relief model of the Thera group. This showed the submerged structure and contours of the caldera. Traces of channels were distinctly visible on its floor. The channels are the same width as the three water rings of the Metropolis. They are as far from the volcanic cone (now the Kameni) as Plato says the rings are from the acropolis. Most surprising of all is a long, deep gorge on the caldera floor. Its length is the same as that of the ship canal, which runs from the sea to the outer ring of water.

The presence of these channels indicated to Galanopoulos that when Thera was a single round island, there could have been natural rings of land and water in its center. The acropolis would have been the cone itself. For centuries in prehistoric time the dormant volcano offered no threat to human life. It would have appeared to be a small hill surrounded by valleys. Had these been below sea level and filled with water, they would have looked like circular bands of water around a domelike hill.

Each time Galanopoulos stated one of the conclusions he drew from the evidence, he offered it as a possibility—just that and no more. Many of his colleagues found, as he listed them, that the similarities between ancient Thera and the Metropolis of Atlantis were many, some so striking that they could not be called accidental.

But the fertile plain was a different matter. Even with its size reduced by a factor of ten, it remained too large by any measure or imaginative stretch to have been part of Thera. Before the eruption the island was only twelve miles in diameter.

Where, then, was the fertile plain located?

Without an answer to that question, the riddle was only partly solved, the theory incomplete.

XX

He Wouldn't Say "No"

❧ Central Crete has a level region of good farmland called the Mesara Plain. Its shape is oblong. The mountains that enclose it on three sides reach south to the open sea, shielding it from the north wind. It is just one-tenth the size of the fertile plain of Atlantis, so that even its dimensions fit Plato's description—if allowance is made for that troublesome tenfold error. Could this be the same region?

Galanopoulos thought so, yes. To explain why, he referred to a sentence in Plato's story that speaks of the "great and marvellous power" of the Atlantean kings, who ruled over "the entire island, many other islands as well, and parts of the continent." These words can mean only that Atlantis includes *several* islands. If Thera is one of them, neighboring Crete is surely another.

The Egyptians made no distinction between the two because they knew of none. And it was their story, after all, that Plato retold. Galanopoulos liked to emphasize this as a major premise of his theory. To the Egyptians, the friendly traders from the west were known as the Keftians, and the name embraced Therans and Cretans alike.

Plato's description of "the Royal City" in relation to the fertile plain has always had one traditional interpretation: that the city and the plain together make up the whole kingdom of Atlantis. By "the Royal City" everyone has assumed that Plato means the circular Metropolis and outer city. Galanopoulos was prepared to challenge this assumption.

In keeping with the tradition, any diagrams or drawings that represent "Atlantis according to Plato" look very much alike. They show that the great wall of the outer city almost touches, or does in fact touch, the south section of the long canal around the plain at its midpoint.

But, said Galanopoulos, the Metropolis and outer city couldn't be "the Royal City." His reason? Even with the fertile plain's dimensions reduced by ten, it never could have been on Thera. Before the eruption Thera was simply too small to contain it.

The tenfold error was proving to be a valuable instrument when he used it on the problems of Atlantean geography, especially this one. The political organization of the kingdom strengthened his argument.

Plato's Atlantis consists of ten districts, each ruled by a king. Presumably there is "a Royal City" for every king: *ten cities.* For each city a fine palace: *ten palaces.* Archaeologists know that Minoan Crete had many others, and prosperous towns grew up around them.

The Mesara plain lies too far south to be "near" Knossos, the most populous of Crete's Bronze Age cities. But Phaistos was another splendid palace. Its impressive ruins are in the Mesara plain.

Then Atlantis does have its fertile plain and "a Royal City" in the same area. The same mountains protect them. *Plain, city, and mountains are in Crete!*

To locate the fertile plain there, said Galanopoulos, is not to lessen the importance of Thera's Metropolis. That could have been a religious center, while Phaistos was the residence of the governor who ruled over the plain. The new concept is not only more logical than the traditional one, it has the evidence of geological and human history behind it.

Nothing about Atlantis has caused more confusion than its supposed location in the Atlantic Ocean. Galanopoulos again put the blame on the tenfold error. Plato certainly knew that the dimensions Solon gave for the plain were wildly out of proportion to the size of the Aegean Sea. He had to respect Solon's belief that the story was true, or else dismiss it entirely. His decision must have been to take Solon at his word, and he deliberately moved Atlantis into the unexplored ocean.

The Greeks of Plato's time knew little about the Minoans except for the misty legends and myths that survived them. Like the Maya of Yucatan, they were a forgotten people. The tale had become a mixture of fact and rumor long before Solon heard it.

Then Plato reshaped it into a dramatic story that would appeal to every Greek's pride of country. His ideal Athenians fight alone against a corrupt enemy. The final destruction of Atlantis adds a harsh moral to the tale. After the twentieth century rediscovered the Minoans, and when modern science began to recognize the impact of the eruption, it finally became possible to separate the fantasy elements from the core of truth hidden within the classic story.

Galanopoulos often pointed out the similarities between Minoan Crete and Atlantis. In a book written with Edward Bacon, *Atlantis: The Truth behind the Legend* (1969), he showed the striking resemblance between the kings of Atlantis and the provincial governors of Crete. The Minoans had one supreme priest-king whose central power base was Knossos, where he lived. He also seems to have been the religious overlord, like the eldest brother to whom the other nine owed their allegiance. The governors, who were all-powerful in their separate districts, worked out mutual defense agreements to secure the peace at home.

Crete resembled Atlantis in having rich resources in its forests. As long ago as 2400 B.C. its shipyards turned out the fast, sturdy vessels that gave the Minoans their control of the seas. They did not lose it until the eruption destroyed their fleet along with their harbors. Its after-effects spoiled their land.

During that thousand-year period, Minoan craftsmen became expert workers in metal. At first their trade was chiefly in products made of copper and bronze—like the swords, daggers, and the little saw found by the young French excavators; later it appears that they also produced gold jewelry.

The military organization of Atlantis, on the other hand, resembles Sparta's. Spartan men received grants of land in return for army service. The weapons and chariots Plato carefully lists are very like those of Spartan warriors.

Homer's heroes relied on just such weapons in the Trojan War.

Galanopoulos traced other links to Atlantis in Minoan art. The bull is featured in the murals and pottery discovered at Knossos. So, too, it is a sacred animal in Atlantis. The kings' elaborate capture of the bull is part of the solemn ceremony when they assemble. It is caught with a noose—no metal weapon may touch it. Then come its sacrifice and their exchange of vows. The robes they wear are dyed the same deep blue, the color of royalty, as the clothing of the priest-king in Knossian frescoes. That valuable blue dye was manufactured in Crete.

Another favorite subject of their artists was the playful dolphin, shown so frequently on their painted pottery. Plato says that inside Poseidon's temple a hundred statues of sea nymphs on dolphins surround the huge gold figure of the sea god.

The imaginary Atlanteans hardly outdo the Minoans in constructing baths and bathing areas, although the open-air baths of Atlantis are much more lavish than anything the Minoans attempted. Still, they were the first people of the ancient world to pipe fresh water directly into buildings. At Knossos the queen enjoyed her own elaborate bathroom, and special bathing rooms were set aside for the use of travel-weary visitors.

Galanopoulos saw other parallels in the achievements of Atlantean designers and craftsmen. Plato mentions the colors of stone used in their buildings. The same hues of red, black, and white are typical of Theran stone, as the island's weathered cliffs reveal today.

It was 1960 when Galanopoulos first identified the great eruption with the sinking of Atlantis. He was soon identifying Minoan Crete *and* Thera with Atlantis, for reasons that he said were "so strong as to be unanswerable." The attitude of many earth scientists was nicely summed up by one of them who wrote, "The case is no more provable than any others yet offered, but is much more plausible than many another to date, and at least it is less *disprovable* than most." That is the judgment of Dr. Dorothy Vitaliano. As a professional geologist she has thoroughly studied all aspects of his theory.

Galanopoulos put it this way: "The solution of this riddle is as simple as the mistake which created it." His modest comment overlooks the years he invested in analysis and research.

In the meantime, events had moved so rapidly that the first archaeological expedition of the twentieth century was actually working at Thera in 1967. Two unrelated happenings helped to bring it about.

The first was a report by two geologists of Columbia University's Lamont Observatory. In 1965, Professors Heezen and Ninkovich published the results of tests made on samples of soft rock and mud drilled from the bed of the Aegean Sea. One layer was composed of ash from an eruption of Thera. By their estimate it had occurred in 1500 or 1400 B.C., and winds had blown the ash more than four hundred miles (700 km) from the volcano. Both men agreed with Galanopoulos that this finding connected the Theran upheavals to the various Bronze Age legends and traditions about sinkings and deluges. Here at last was the sort of objective evidence that Aegean archaeologists had been eager to see. They were delighted with it. There was a surge of interest in Thera. The island was long overdue for intensive investigation.

By another coincidence it was also 1965 when an American naval engineer was in Athens. He met Professor Galanopoulos and discussed his Thera-Atlantis ideas with him. James W. Mavor, Jr., became the driving force behind an ambitious plan to organize a full-scale study of Thera. He hoped to enlist scientists from several fields, then to make underwater surveys of the caldera while archaeologists and technical specialists concentrated on the island.

The first exploratory digging was planned for 1967. Suitably enough, it would begin exactly one hundred years after Fouqué made his historic finds. The man who agreed to direct the project was Dr. Spyridon Marinatos. His early theory about the drastic effects of the eruption on Crete had all but died of neglect. For twenty years he had done archaeological field work in Crete and was a leading authority on the Minoans. He had made a survey of Thera in 1962. During a second visit two years after that he decided that the logical place to excavate, when the time came, was the region near Akrotiri.

By 1967, Marinatos was Inspector General of the Greek Antiquities Service. He led the campaigns at Thera for six seasons, uncovering the fragile ruins of a prosperous Minoan city. Houses two and three storeys high were found under layers of ash and pumice. In some of them were frescoes as gracious and beautiful as those so fleetingly seen a century earlier by the young French scholars. Thanks to modern techniques, a good many were saved.

The first news reports of spectacular discoveries were often headlined "LOST ATLANTIS FOUND!" When Marinatos was asked if the little island really was Atlantis, he never insisted that it was. Sometimes he answered with a smile and sometimes with an impatient shrug; he was always cautious about extravagant claims. But he did not make an outright denial, either. Not in so many words. He would tell questioners that in modern Greek the word *legend* means ". . . something mixed of historic and imaginary elements, and above all, something which became a glorious but dubious tradition." Even in so many words, that doesn't sound like "No."

The man, the place, and the legend had finally met. What he saw as a young man working at Amnisos had brought them together.

XXI

"Bull's-Eye"

The most promising and least dangerous place to excavate at Thera was a field near Akrotiri. Marinatos knew that much in advance. Centuries of wind and rain have lowered the layers of volcanic ash here by as much as sixty-five feet. The French found pre-eruption pottery and tools in this area, and somewhere nearby were the buried houses they explored. But these discoveries were always made by accident.

The village of Akrotiri stands on the southern tip of the crescent-shaped island. In clear weather one can see Crete outlined against the southern horizon. Marinatos told himself that Minoan colonists would have built their homes within sight of the motherland. That, too, influenced his choice.

The opportunity had finally come to test his belief that

the eruption ruined Crete's soil and forced its palaces to be abandoned forever. The truth must lie here on Thera, concealed under tons of volcanic waste.

Spades and picks cut into the dusty ground one hot morning in May of 1967. The first trench was on the west side of a large ravine. It was a dry gully in summer, but every winter it filled with rainwater to become a torrent.

With Marinatos, besides a crew of Greek workmen, was Mrs. Emily Vermeule, a research fellow of the Boston Museum of Fine Arts, a classics scholar and professor of Greek and art. They were friends of long standing. Mavor was also present. For him, the excavation would test the Galanopoulos theory that ancient Thera was the Metropolis and outer city of Atlantis. Several people who had volunteered as technical advisers were standing by when the work began.

Friends from Mavor's home base in Massachusetts, the Woods Hole Oceanographic Institution, had recently helped him use special instruments aboard an American research ship while it was in Aegean waters. He took deep-sea cores from the caldera bottom and made a "map" of its floor with a sonar device. The results indicated that Thera once contained a deep harbor and winding inner bays. It was not possible to say whether they were circular, like those of Atlantis, but he was pleased and encouraged.

Within hours Marinatos was handling fragments of painted jars, found on the site only three feet below the surface. They were made in Crete, he said, between 1520 and 1500 B.C. This was gratifying: it gave him a firm date to work with. What strides archaeology had taken in one century! The types of potsherds that had baffled the French he could identify instantly.

A mass of loose stones slowed the digging for a while—all this on the first day—before they were recognized as caved-in walls. One clay cup and a stone lamp were found. The lamp was still black with soot as though its flame had been snuffed out suddenly.

When upright walls were found near the loose stones, Marinatos sensed that he might be on the upper floor of a house. He ordered the trench closed to protect the interior and whatever might be in it. By digging to the north and tunneling, the crew could search for the outer walls.

The move was either lucky or inspired. The next day they uncovered the limestone front of a house imposing enough to be called a small palace. After a doorway was cleared it was plain to see that *in architecture and construction this was a Minoan building.* They dug no deeper, because the door could very well be on a second storey. To probe for a lower level was too risky.

The way the upper walls had collapsed was an early clue to what happened during the disaster. According to geologists, earthquakes do not occur during an eruption. The whole ruin was covered with white ash, but when he searched beneath the pile of stones Marinatos could find no ash at all, which meant that the structure was demolished by a heavy quake or quakes *before* it was smothered under pumice and ash. This was a valuable finding in itself.

Pumice is the material first discharged from an erupting volcano of Thera's type, and on Thera it forms a pebbly layer about four feet thick, pink and gray in color. Above this ribbonlike band lies the enormous deposit of ash, sixty to seventy feet thick and in places as thick as one hundred and fifty feet. The ash consists of particles of pure white glass crystals, very soft and so light that it can be dug out by hand. In fact, the last steps in clearing were by hand, then with fine brushes.

A second trench was opened at the mouth of a cave east of the ravine, less than three hundred feet from the first one. An old villager remembered that years ago part of the cave floor fell in. What looked like the room of a buried house could be seen when one peered into the inky blackness below. A local tradition like this was worth investigating. The section where the first trench went down was called Bronos, in honor of the field's owner. For the same reason the second section excavated was named Arvanitis, after the family who owned it.

Late that afternoon two limestone walls appeared at a depth of six feet in the new trench. A broad, hand-cut windowframe was built into one of them. On the thin stone slabs of its sill were groove marks showing where double swinging sashes had hung, to open and close at the touch of some Theran who lived here thirty-five hundred years ago. The wooden frame had vanished because the ash was fiery hot when it fell; the wood actually evaporated. But its exact shape was clearly imprinted in the ash. This building, like the first, had more than one storey. Tests made in two other trenches revealed houses close to it. Tradition was correct! The cave was man-made, carved out of a bank of pumice and ash, and underneath it was an ancient house.

"We hit the bull's-eye right away," said Marinatos, recalling the excitement of those hours. "We struck at the heart of the most aristocratic quarter."

They had found a city. The first five days of what was planned to be a preliminary excavation were a stunning success. To see Minoan houses still standing, to realize that they were two, perhaps three storeys tall, was an experience without parallel. Many palaces in Crete are little more than traces of low, eroded walls and the outlines of rooms. The volcano that shattered the island of Thera had preserved these houses in its ash.

In no sense of the word was this an ordinary site. Everyone involved was keenly aware that they were at work not in a primitive settlement but an affluent Minoan city of the sixteenth century before Christ. No one could guess how deep the digging might go. One test hole ran fifteen feet straight down through ash and pumice before stone walls were detected. And no one could predict the city's extent.

Once open to the air, every square foot that was excavated needed protective roofing against winter storms. Bulldozers and other kinds of heavy earth-moving machines would be essential. How else move the ash to the sea? And that would mean a new harbor, paved roads . . .

There was much to do each afternoon when the digging stopped. The yield of pottery, broken or whole, was extremely rich. Many objects had been made locally, but there were imported pieces as well. Lists of household items grew longer and longer. The smallest potsherds were gently sorted and cleaned. Along with other valuable finds they were carefully placed in baskets lined with grass and taken to the museum at Phirá, traveling the ten miles over the narrow, hilly road on the backs of donkeys. Mrs. Vermeule and several assistants made photographs, plans, and drawings of each newly excavated area. Mavor was using his cameras to keep a photographic record of day-to-day activities.

The funds raised for the work fell alarmingly short of what was required for the present season. Extraordinary methods would have to be devised to prevent slides and cave-ins. This would be the responsibility of engineers and mining specialists.

Work stopped for three weeks while Marinatos went to Athens. Other duties claimed his attention, and he wanted to get official government permission to go on digging because the site was on private property.

The Americans had only one week of their own time remaining when he returned. The money problem was not solved. For the present the work force—most of them were village men from Akrotiri—was augmented by forty. The owner of a local pumice mine paid their wages. Their skill and confidence were reassuring to the whole crew, because the miners were old hands at moving powdery ash. Coping with unstable banks of pumice was all part of a day's work to them. Volcanic boulders sometimes impeded the digging. Chunks of lava weighing a ton or more had been hurled thousands of feet from the exploding crater. Removing them was a sweaty job and time-consuming.

The word was getting around that some strange and very old things (houses, they said) were being found near Akrotiri. Older folk and children with their dogs trotting after them came from other villages to have a look at the site. They enjoyed seeing so many foreigners (important people, they said) making long ditches and holes in the ground near Akrotiri. Close to the tomato fields and grapevines, too. It was something to watch and it made you wonder, all this digging. But it stirred up plenty of dust; you could tell where they were before you even got there, because they made white dust blow all over everything. It turned your dark clothes white in no time. Why, the men working there looked like ghosts.

By mid-June seven new trenches were opened, making nine in all. Each ran at an angle of ninety degrees from the ravine. Another success like that of the first week was too much to expect, and no one did. But it happened. This time they found a house of either two or three storeys, with traces of fresco paintings on the interior walls.

XXII

Trials and Rewards

The men working a new trench in the Bronos sector saw it first: a painted wall. Others soon emerged from the ash. Bits of colored plaster as well as large pieces were scattered among domestic wares like cups and cooking pots. On some walls fair-sized segments of frescoes were still in place.

There is no record that anyone except Mamet and Gorceix had ever seen a Theran wall-painting. But here were others, and with the help of expert art restorers they might be saved. Their colors were clear but not the designs. Because this house was closer to the surface, it had been more vulnerable to erosion than the one the young Frenchmen entered by tunneling.

Some frescoes were black against white backgrounds. Reds, pinks, and greens were the prevailing colors. New

designs had been applied here and there over earlier paintings, as though the home owner had decided to redecorate.
All of them faded slightly during the first hours of being
in the open air, but no more after that.

Two doors could be recognized. One opened onto a
flagstone floor that was still in place, although it sloped
sharply toward the center of the room. The lower, or
basement level of the house could not be entered because
its walls had been weakened by water seepage; the men
were taking no risks.

How were the frescoes to be saved? Time was running
out. An art technician hurried from Athens for a conference. In the end the reluctant decision was made to
close the trench. The delicate job of salvaging the paintings had to wait until it could be done properly, and that
would not be for another year. At least their presence in
one part of the site could mean that other frescoes would
be discovered.

The finds made during the last few days bore out the
early impression that the team was working in an aristocratic quarter of the city. Ash was cleared from the front
of another large house built of well-cut limestone blocks.
It seemed to overlook an open courtyard. Only master
masons could have cut stone so well, and only a person
of great means could have afforded a mansion as grand as
this.

In the Arvanitis sector the workmen were able to enter
a basement-level room where a row of large storage jars
was still standing upright. Each was three feet tall. Near
them was a low, square kitchen hearth surrounded by
cooking utensils. A stone mortar with its grinding stone
lay beside it. Adjoining rooms were found later, so that

the basement level turned out to be a three-part storeroom containing a wide variety of extremely rare vases and unique types of pottery. The row of large jars was held firmly in place by pumice, which had acted as packing material and helped to protect them. They were unbroken but their surfaces were cracked as if from extreme heat.

The study of each excavated house was giving the team important new information about Minoan construction methods. The walls of upper storeys were commonly made of mud bricks, reinforced with wooden beams or saplings —the earliest known example of a deliberate attempt at earthquake-proofing.

It seemed that with each discovery, a new problem

Minoan storage jars being removed from pumice and ash.
(Photograph by Mary Alice Keir.)

presented itself. The team was frequently at a loss to know whether they had reached the upper or the lower level of a building; floors and walls had been wrenched out of place by one or several earthquakes. The result was a bewildering subsurface maze. Whenever Marinatos faced this situation, he decided against trying to dig deeper or tunnel through to the interior of a house; they were unprepared for such complicated work this season.

To add one more problem to the rest, they were learning what widespread damage had been caused by the heavy flow of water that raced through the bed of the ravine each winter. For untold years it had been seeping into the foundations and rooms of buildings under its bed and near its banks. "The torrent," as Marinatos called it, would have to be controlled, which would require the construction of a new channel for it, and as soon as possible.

In spite of every difficulty it was still true that the houses and their contents reflected the tastes and the varied talents of people who resided in a prosperous community. Their lives had been violently interrupted. There was a curious absence of gold objects or jewelry and even of simple metal tools. The only bones identified were those of domestic animals. The French had much the same experience a century ago, although they had come upon one human skeleton. It appeared that the earthquake activity was alarming enough to drive most of the city dwellers away, carrying their most valuable possessions with them. Anything too heavy to carry had been left behind.

There were some indications, though, that a few had either stayed on or had returned to Thera before the eruption. Stark and dramatic proof of that came to light during another summer of excavation.

Before the 1967 season ended, Marinatos spoke of wanting to make the site into a living museum. He was looking far into the future with his hope that the ancient buildings could be preserved exactly as they were found, but protected under a strongly supported roof of pumice. Then the people of modern Thera could work their fields and vineyards overhead while visitors to the museum walked through the prehistoric streets below. It was a bold plan and perhaps it was beyond realization; but to turn a dream so daring into reality would create an archaeological showplace unlike any other in the world.

Everything would depend on how securely its protective "shell" of pumice could be reinforced. On this earthquake-prone volcanic island, it would have to be made safe or not even attempted. Marinatos was concerned about the future of the land. He foresaw the day when the fields planted with tomatoes and wine grapes might have to give way to the site as the excavations progressed. The ideal "living museum" he envisioned would not interfere with the harvesting of the villagers' major crops. It would allow the remote past and the ongoing present to live harmoniously together.

Before the 1968 dig could even begin, however, large sums of money were required. Provision had to be made for the art restorers and for the architects and technical consultants he wanted to recruit. Preferably, they should have living quarters near the site. It would be a formidable undertaking.

James Mavor came to a firm conclusion before he left for home that summer. What they had already found of the still nameless city qualified it, he thought, to be called Atlantis. He believed that the Galanopoulos theory was proving to be correct in the most significant respects. The evidence at hand convinced Mavor that Thera was the Metropolis and outer city of Plato's lost kingdom.

Dr. Marinatos was more cautious. He would go so far as to say that after the eruption the Egyptians lost all contact with Crete. Then, learning later that a rich and powerful island kingdom had disappeared into the sea, they assumed that Crete had vanished. This is exactly what Marinatos had believed for years, and he was not about to change his opinion with the excavation in its earliest stage. Yes, the Atlantis story probably originated with the Egyptians; he would grant Plato that. And the volcanic destruction of Thera was probably the core of the Atlantis story. So, also, was a great number of myths and legends that grew out of the widespread effects of that disaster. He let it be understood, however, that he thought it was too early to speculate on Atlantis or to draw premature conclusions about this Minoan city, whose size was still unknown.

Mrs. Vermeule took a middle course, feeling as she did that it was far less important to identify Thera with Atlantis than to recognize that for the first time in history an authentic Minoan settlement had been reclaimed. It was an understandable difference of opinion among people who in the course of a few weeks had shared the labor as well as the trials and rewards of a successful dig. It seemed to each one of them a much longer time than that since the first trial trench was opened in May.

The Americans departed. Marinatos raised enough money in grants from his government to extend the work for a while longer, but the 1967 season was over when every trench was closed and the most valuable sections of the site, like the large storeroom with its row of tall jars, were individually roofed and sealed. They were made safe from the ravages of weather and one other agent of destruction: the ruthless vandal, who is a menace to any unguarded archaeological site.

XXIII

Each Is a Promise

The discovery of a Minoan city buried on a volcanic island was news. It was the rumored link to Plato's lost kingdom that transformed it into headlines. When reporters for the news services mentioned the magic word *Atlantis,* their stories took on the flavor of science fiction. Anyone familiar with the legend's history could predict what would happen next.

A strange assortment of people immediately raised protests and denials. By their own admission they were the authorities on Atlantis. Reporters found them united only in their scorn for the suggestion that Thera had any connection with the *real* Atlantis. Depending on who was interviewed, they named the places where they *knew,* they could *prove,* it actually was.

The list held no surprises: Yucatán, Egypt, the Azores.

Each place name revealed which quaint old theory was being fiercely defended, and some new ones joined the list. Spain did, and for some obscure reason, Ireland. Scuba divers who had been prowling around on the ocean floor near the Bahama Islands came to the surface with word that they had sighted a broken marble column, like the pillar of a Greek temple, which meant that Atlantis had to be right *there*.

Earth scientists and archaeologists were restrained in their comments. Akrotiri, not Atlantis, held their attention. Professor Galanopoulos had been following developments at Thera with understandable relish. His theory, he said, was standing up to every test; he was happy to let the facts and the findings speak for themselves.

One person who refused to join the international argument was Dr. Marinatos. He had already expressed himself on the Atlantis matter. At present he was too busy preparing for the second season at Akrotiri to say much for publication, except that it was too early to say anything at all.

With a financial grant from the Greek government he could start the 1968 season in June by making improvements on the site. Other grants followed. The excavation of the prehistoric town was quickly recognized as one of the most important archaeological undertakings of the century.

No new digging would be done until the ruins discovered last year were given protective cover. Otherwise, a single heavy rainstorm would destroy them as soon as they were exposed to the weather.

The technical work began in June. First the torrent in the ravine was tamed. A concrete-lined trench altered its course to carry the heavy winter run-off southward and away from the very heart of the site. Next, the ruins were enclosed with permanent roofing and sidewalls. A huge shed-like structure was erected, supported by steel pillars anchored in solid bedrock. Year after year as the excavated areas gradually increased in size, the shed was to become impressively large.

The conventional method of excavating is to open from the surface and dig down to uncover a buried ruin. But Marinatos and his staff were contending with deep, unstable layers of volcanic material. Erosion had simplified their task only in one section: along and under the bed of the torrent. Everywhere else the problem was to reach whatever lay beneath embankments of pumice and ash without danger to the workmen or further damage to the ruins. The stones of some walls had been made brittle by hot falling pumice.

Radically new methods of excavation were developed. Whenever buried walls were detected, ash was removed until their outlines were clear. The area above them was immediately placed under cover. Up went the steel pillars and the prefabricated roofing to shelter them. Sometimes the crew tunneled on either side of the shelter and tediously worked their way toward the walls of any nearby structures. The long tunnels, or galleries, were then securely braced and digging continued underground. This slow but successful method was less dangerous than it sounds.

A laboratory was built for the artist-restorers. Many of them were young men and women students from the Athens School of Restoration. Eventually as many as forty would be in residence at one time, learning to reconstruct frescoes and mend pottery under the direction of artists and master technicians.

The "living museum" idea underwent changes but the plan Marinatos finally adopted had the same objectives. No excavator had the right, he said, to destroy the picture of life that was "captured within the ruins by the sudden catastrophe." He wanted everything to remain where it was found. Priceless objects would go to museums. No museum, however, could convey the terrible reality of a stricken city deserted by its residents. As he said, "We decided to excavate not a ruin but a museum."

The site became his entire focus of concern and concentration. Since no further oceanographic studies were considered, James Mavor did not return to Thera, but without his initial enthusiasm and initiative the now-famous discoveries of 1967 could have been delayed for years.

Famous they certainly were, to judge by a steep rise in the number of tourists. It was one thing for the Therans, who today make up a population of seven thousand, to hear that the dusty ruins were part of a big town where perhaps as many as twenty-five thousand people had once lived. But that strangers would travel so far just to have a look at them—that was incredible.

The island's main hotel had survived the 1956 earthquake and was proudly named the Atlantis. It seldom had vacancies. When the actual digging was resumed in July, Marinatos posted a guard at the main entrance to the site with orders to see that visiting hours were respected.

Mrs. Vermeule returned to Akrotiri and took personal charge of reopening the house where the first fresco pieces were found. Its flagstone-paved second floor and the interior stone staircase leading to it from the lower level were fully explored. What Marinatos described as a "wealth" of pottery was recovered, some vases and jars broken but others in good condition. Among new-found fresco fragments was one showing the head of a blue monkey, an animated creature with a big brown eye and white muzzle, the most striking piece yet seen. Hopes went soaring again. Where was the rest of the painting? Did it belong in this house or had the torrent carried it here from some building farther north?

Water damage to the foundation walls was extensive, so that for the second time they had to give up the attempt to enter the basement. This was disappointing, as they were eager to determine whether the structures on either side of the torrent had been one large building or many separate units. At least the excavators were now certain that this house consisted of three storeys: a lower floor or basement, a second floor tiled with flagstones, and an upper room.

To clear any room took long hours of labor. Everything it contained was photographed or diagrammed in place; none of the volcanic dust was discarded until it had been sifted to make sure that no small items were overlooked. Each detail of the interior and exterior construction of rooms and buildings was recorded.

Work in the Arvanitis sector, to the north, led to a series of dramatic discoveries. The three-part storeroom had a floor space of 480 square feet, most of it covered with pumice. The team did not know until the pumice was removed that it concealed a collection of rare ceramic wares and household utensils.

On the heels of this exciting find came another. There

were apartments above the storeroom. They and the storeroom were only part of a large complex of buildings. One
upper room had been a Minoan shrine. A ground-floor
entryway with a stone bench still in place was separated
from the storeroom by a double wall. It gave access to a
larger room where they found the upper and lower grindstones of a mill, complete and undisturbed.

Here, said Marinatos, either the king or the high priests
ground flour to make loaves of bread as offerings to their
gods. The arrangement of rooms resembled those in several Cretan palaces which were set apart for religious
rituals. The Mill House, as it was promptly named, was
the center of a religious sanctuary.

Certain choice objects in this area helped to identify
the special character of the shrine room. One was a
painted plaster chest in which incense or herbs were stored.
It was clear from the design of a small table that it held
offerings. Another prize vessel was a rhyton, a ceremonial
drinking cup, beautifully fashioned in the shape of a lion's
head. Eroded fragments of alabaster were all that remained of a delicate chalice.

The fresco pieces were as distinctive as the ritual objects. One showed an altar with columns and "the horns
of consecration." The horns were a symbol of the sacred
bull of Knossos and also symbolized the Minoan empire.
Several broken pieces seemed to be from a landscape in
which colorful birds and flowers were pictured in realistic
detail. The original location of the blue monkey fresco
was becoming a fascinating puzzle. Small fragments
painted with parts of monkeys' bodies were recovered;
they were unmistakably the work of one artist.

Scenes of disorder often confronted the excavators

when the ash was cleared and they could at last get inside
a buried building. Pottery lay in heaps, indicating that it
had dropped from the upper rooms of a house when the
floors fell in, or tumbled from shelves and niches in walls.
The only trace of wooden shelving was the imprint it left
in the surrounding pumice. Walls slanted away from the
perpendicular. Steps were wrenched apart in well-built
stone stairways.

They were grim reminders that the city suffered two
distinct blows. The first was dealt by earthquake. It shook
down the mud-brick walls and roofs of upper storeys. The
second blow came from the eruption. How long the time
interval was between the two, Marinatos could not say;
that was for geologists and volcanologists to decide. But
he could testify that when the rain of pumice and ash
began, it poured down on empty streets and roofless
houses. Pumice invaded their interiors before the buildings
themselves were smothered in ash.

The city extended farther both north and south than
anyone anticipated. Its ruins were twenty to forty feet
below the surface, or unpredictably deeper. Even so, Marinatos believed that its north end crashed into the caldera
in the last phase of the eruption. As though to confirm
this belief, a few seasons later one of the sites Mamet and
Gorceix explored in 1870 was rediscovered after long
searching. It was the same ruined house on the cliffs northwest of Akrotiri village that was torn in half when the
sea swallowed the center of the island.

Fresh signs of the disaster were uncovered from time
to time as the excavations progressed. It was a moving
experience for staff members to enter rooms sealed away
in darkness and there find themselves face to face with

mute evidence of what the forces of destruction had done. To come upon little common things people left behind or dropped in their flight—a fishhook, a broken flowerpot—this could not fail to touch the finder's heart.

Marinatos became bitterly angry one day when a tourist stole some loom weights, the sort women used in weaving cloth. In his eyes the theft was worse than vandalism. It was like profaning a holy sanctuary, and he tightened the already strict security measures.

The artifacts recovered in the 1968 season included the first bronze sickles, nails, and hooks, and a full set of graduated lead weights, like those used in balance scales today. The inventory of vases and jars was lengthy. Many were variations of types familiar to archaeologists, though some were unique. One large jar defied classification. It had a lid and a perforated floor over its base, with a small door that opened and closed just above the base. Almost ten years later it was identified as a beehive, the earliest ever found.

Among the household items was a large lamp collection. There were mortars and grinders of many sizes, cooking utensils, and ceramic pots with built-in strainers. A miniature bathtub of terra cotta was either a child's toy or a cradle. Small round objects of clay or stone were recognized as "jackstones," used in a children's game; others, differently shaped, Marinatos thought could be pieces from an ancient chess set.

After a preliminary study of the imported pottery, Marinatos could say that Thera traded not just with Crete but with many islands of the Greek Aegean. None of the pottery was made later than 1500 B.C. Here was another firm date by which to fix the probable time of the earthquake. The shrine and religious center reflected the influence of Cretan culture, although their presence did not necessarily prove that Thera was under Crete's political rule.

When the season ended the entire staff felt assured that the site was safeguarded by every means human ingenuity could contrive. They were still at the outset of a complicated, demanding project that would continue for years. Each new find was gratifying in itself and a promise of many more to come. Marinatos was encouraged by the artistic merit of the fresco fragments, though they were few in number. Unlike material objects, which the ancient Therans could take with them, wall paintings could not be removed. There were, he wrote, "sure indications" that they were hidden in several parts of the area now being excavated. This statement was a prediction. If he had said the paintings would prove to be one of Thera's greatest treasures, he would have been very close to the mark.

The uncanny accuracy of that prediction was borne out the following season, when the first of the lost paintings was found.

XXIV

The Door Opens Wider

🌿 They were clearing pumice from a room in Bronos sector when the excavators uncovered a shapeless mass of stone slabs. It lay where it had dropped when an upper floor collapsed. They were working about thirty feet north of the house where the first fresco pieces had been found two years earlier.

Among the slabs were recognizable fragments of a great wall painting. The chunks of fresco had fallen from the walls of the upper room. By a curious accident, as its floor gave way they became tightly wedged together by the flagstones that covered the floor, and all slid down in one large mass. Enough of the painting survived to be reconstructed.

Almost four years later the art restorers completed their incredibly patient work. They had rediscovered the basic composition of the fresco and assembled its myriad jigsaw-like parts. It was given a place of honor as "The Room of the Blue Monkeys" in the National Museum of Athens.

Here visitors may see monkeys, a troupe of them, scrambling and leaping gracefully over wildflowers and red rocks that resemble the lava outcroppings visible on Thera today. No one knows whether it is an actual land-scape, much less whether monkeys once roamed freely somewhere on the island.

The excavations at Akrotiri have drawn on the skills and the knowledge of artists and art restorers as well as scientists. The Blue Monkey fresco, found in 1969, is a brilliant example of their creative collaboration.

The work schedule for the 1969 season followed an established routine. After technical improvements were made, new excavations began. Warehouses were built for supplies and heavy machines. Residences and workshops were added for members of the staff. Some of them could now work all year under the covering shed. The menders' laboratory expanded again and again and still could barely keep pace with the ceramic finds. By the mid-1970s, there was a small, highly specialized scientific community in the fields near the Bronze Age city.

With the excavated areas steadily enlarging, the site was divided into quarters. Each was assigned a letter of the Greek alphabet. The northern sector, formerly called Arvanitis, was now simply A, or Alpha. The southern sector, first known as Bronos, was divided in half; its eastern part became B, or Beta, while its western half was Γ (Gamma). The area between Alpha and Beta was designated Δ (Delta). Arabic numbers indicated indi-vidual rooms and corridors of excavated buildings. The

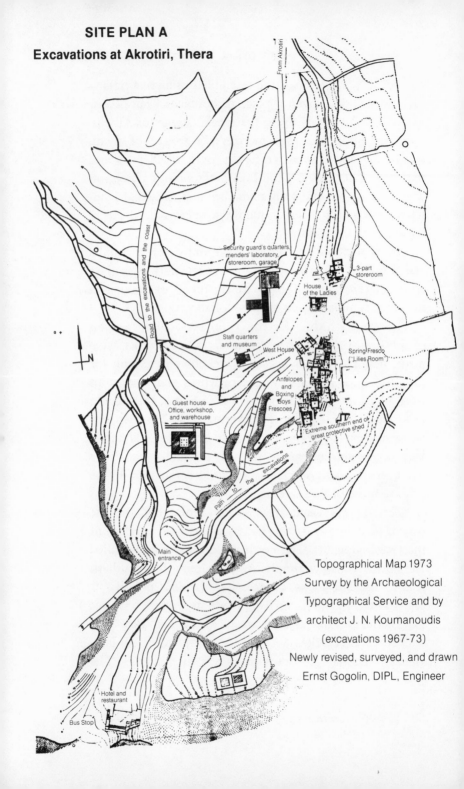

SITE PLAN A

Excavations at Akrotiri, Thera

From Akrotiri

Road to the excavations and the coast

Security guard's quarters, menders' laboratory, storeroom, garage

3-part storeroom

House of the Ladies

N

Staff quarters and museum

West House

Spring Fresco ("Lilies Room")

Antelopes and Boxing Boys Frescoes

Guest house Office, workshop, and warehouse

Extreme southern end of great protective shed

Path to the excavations

Main entrance

Topographical Map 1973
Survey by the Archaeological
Typographical Service and by
architect J. N. Koumanoudis
(excavations 1967-73)
Newly revised, surveyed, and drawn
Ernst Gogolin, DIPL, Engineer

Hotel and restaurant

Bus Stop

first fresco pieces, for instance, appeared in B2. The Blue Monkey fresco was found in B6. Rooms of the three-part storeroom in Alpha sector are A1, A2, and A3. Site Plan B, page 178, shows the mill with its separate entrance in the same building.

The first clear indication of one part of the city's original plan came with the discovery of a long street paved with cobblestones. It ran north between Gamma and Beta sectors to an open couryard or small public square, which was called Courtyard 1 or North Court. But here the street was partly blocked by heaps of fallen building stones and decayed mud bricks shaken down by the earthquake. Before that, as the glassy smoothness of its worn surface showed, it had been a busy thoroughfare.

What the team found next came as a complete surprise. In the period of time between the seismic disaster and the eruption, a few survivors had taken refuge in deserted buildings along the street. The city was already in partial ruin. Upper storeys of many buildings had crumbled. The "squatters," as Marinatos termed them, had to crawl to and from their basement rooms through ground-level windows because doorways were choked with debris. They heaped up barricades of fallen stones to keep walls from collapsing in the buildings they occupied, and they managed even to clear rubble from the street. It was still possible to see the footpath they made through the ruins.

"Squatters" was the word Sir Arthur Evans used to describe the desperate people who stayed on at Knossos after it was gutted by fire. Marinatos had them in mind constantly as the evidence came to light that a few Theran survivors put up a valiant struggle to keep alive after the earthquake.

Site Plan A: *Contour map of excavation, 1973.* (Courtesy of Archaeological Society of Athens.)

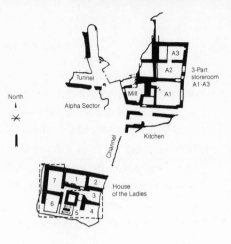

SITE PLAN B
Excavations at Akrotiri, Thera
General Typography
Sectors A, B, Γ, Δ   Thera 1973
Architect: I. N. Koumanoudis

North

Alpha Sector

Tunnel

Mill

A3
A2
A1

3-Part
storeroom
A1-A3

Channel

Kitchen

House
of the Ladies

7 1 2
6   3
5 4

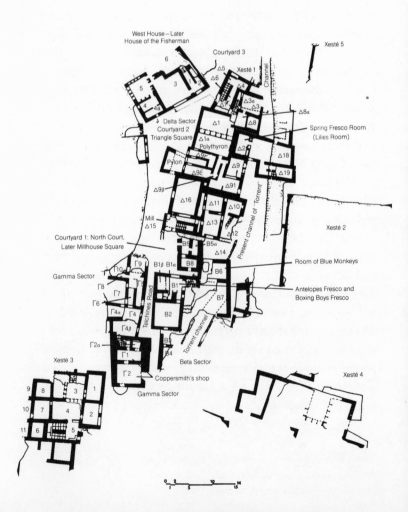

West House — Later
House of the Fisherman

Courtyard 3

Xesté 5

6

Δ5
Δ6

Xesté 1

5   3   2
4
4a

Δ4
Δ3a
Δ3

Channel

Δ8a

Delta Sector
Courtyard 2
Triangle Square

Δ1
Δ1a

Δ8

Spring Fresco Room
(Lilies Room)

Polythyron

Δ2

Pylon

Δ9γ
Δ9ε

Δ9
Δ91

Δ18
Δ19

Δ9β

Δ16

Δ11
Δ13

Δ10

Present channel of "Torrent"

Mill
Δ15

Δ12

Xesté 2

Courtyard 1: North Court,
Later Millhouse Square

Δ14

B9
B5a

B1β B1a
B8
B6

Room of Blue Monkeys

Γ9
Γ10

Gamma Sector

Γ8

B1

Antelopes Fresco and
Boxing Boys Fresco

Γ7
Γ6

Γ4a Γ4

B2

B7

Γ4β

Γ2a

B3
B4

Xesté 3

Γ1

Γ2

Torrent channel

Beta Sector

Coppersmith's shop

Gamma Sector

9 8   3   1
10 7   4   2
11 6   5

Xesté 4

0   2   10   M
 1   5   15

In the long process of reopening the street, the team learned that the squatters had turned two rooms—Gamma 1 and 2—into temporary metalwork shops. This is why it was named the Telchines (těl KĪN ēs) Road. In Greek mythology the Telchines were an ancient people who were given credit for inventing the craft of metalworking.

Little hoards of food were found in many rooms. Analysis revealed that beans stored in jars had sprouted and certain seeds had germinated before volcanic pumice began to fall.

The wholly unexpected findings convinced Marinatos that the time between earthquake and eruption was very brief, contrary to what he had believed. At the most, not more than three years elapsed, but more probably it was only a few months before the survivors were driven out when the volcano roared into life. Why had they stayed? He supposed that they were searching for their dead or for lost belongings, and he revised his estimate of the date for the eruption: Thera's end came between 1520 and 1500 B.C. In another twenty years Crete was a desolate island. Earthquakes and tsunami took their toll, and deposits of air-borne ash had slowly poisoned its good soil.

One last discovery of 1969 opened even wider the once-sealed doorway into Thera's past. Teams working in Beta and Gamma sectors ran into extremely hazardous conditions. *Many buildings had sunk.* During a late phase of the eruption, violent earth movements and shock waves from the exploding volcano compressed their walls. As the ground began to sink, the heavy stone steps of interior stairways were literally squeezed together, as though in a vise, until individual steps split in half. Houses in Gamma, Beta, and also in Delta sectors were so ruined that excava-

Site Plan B: *Plan of the excavation made in 1973.* (Courtesy of Archaeological Society of Athens.)

The southeast corner of North Court, showing the begin-ning of Telchines Road. Note the barricades made by "squatters." (Photograph by Mary Alice Keir.)

---

tion had to stop. It would resume only when their walls could be braced.

While many of these walls were still upright, they were riddled with gaps and breaks. They no longer stood verti-cal but were tilted slightly toward the southeast. Had they not been buried under pumice and ash at the time of the sinking, they would have been leveled to the ground. Traces of fine silt or of river mud and sand were further evidence that they had borne the brunt of the final ex-plosive upheaval.

Even before the first dig in 1967 Marinatos had known that the southern part of the island, including Akrotiri, had undergone a light but perceptible sinking. Thera's southern shoreline is shallow. A layer of pumice lies off-

Broken staircase showing effects of compression and sinking. (Photograph by Mary Alice Keir.)

---

shore, below the present sea-level. These strangely deformed ruins told their own story of the way a proud city perished.

What does Plato say about Atlantis? He shortens its dying to a day and a night. He says there were earthquakes and floods before the island was swallowed by the sea.

For hundreds of years, seafarers passing within sight of Thera would have looked at barren and scarred cliffs where there was no sign of human life. A shroud of ash hid all that remained of the ruined city.

From such disasters and from what is imperfectly remembered about them, legends are made.

XXV

The Prints of Human Lives

🌿 Delta sector was opened in 1970. It was no secret that important ruins were buried in this large unexcavated area. They had been detected in the first trial trench when the dig began. Delta sector reached all the way from Alpha in the north to Beta and Gamma, south.

Marinatos felt well prepared for an arduous undertaking. New methods of tunneling and ways of bracing weakened structures were safe and efficient. The digging crew had earth-moving machines and the other heavy equipment they needed. Progress was good. They were soon working eighteen and twenty feet below the surface of the fields.

Their first discovery was that Delta sector formed a connecting link between the northern and southern extremes of the site. And what a link it was! Nearly every ruin in it was part of one large building, a complex of single rooms and apartments, corridors, anterooms and storage rooms. Until now Beta 1 and 1a were thought to be private houses, but no: they were units of the one dominating structure. More impressive still, in some sections it had been two, three, and possibly four storeys tall, while its length from north to south was 263 feet. For a building of the Bronze Age era it was unprecedented in size and architectural design.

To distinguish it from smaller mansions Marinatos called it a *xesté* (kses TAY). The word describes an exceptionally large building with a facing of hand-cut stone blocks—"ashlar masonry" to the architect. It would take years to excavate Xesté 1 and longer than that to understand what use had been made of its many rooms and suites of rooms. By 1973, the ruins of three others had been located. They appear on Site Plan B, page 178, as Xesté 2 (unexcavated), 3 and 4 (partly excavated). A fifth xesté is not on the plan because it was discovered after 1973.

A word about the two plans, A and B, pages 180 and 178. Both were commissioned in 1973. Site Plan A is a topographical map that gives an overview of the site with its ancient ruins and modern buildings. The contours of the land are shown, along with living quarters for staff, warehouses, laboratories, a newly built museum, and a guest house.

Site Plan B is a detailed drawing of the ruins. Greek letters signify sectors: A, B, Γ, Δ. Numbers indicate individual rooms of buildings and the order in which each was discovered. The small numbered squares show the locations of the steel pillars that support the protective shed.

The most intensive work was now concentrated on the south sectors. The present southern coast of Thera is only a thousand feet from them, although its pre-eruption shoreline was a mile farther south. Marinatos was convinced that he had reached the center of the ancient harbor section. The partial excavation of several independent houses showed that they were the homes of wealthy people, the merchant princes or shipowners and captains of their time.

Again there were buildings trapped in pumice and ash to the level of their second-storey floors. They leaned slightly toward the southeast, tilted in that direction by ferocious blasts from the volcano. The results of sinking and compression were terrible to see. A stone staircase was

View of site from the east, during excavation of Delta sector. (Photograph by Mary Alice Keir.)

discovered in Delta 5. Each step was broken in half, dis-
closing what happened when the ground sank lightly
beneath it. The bottom step has deep scrape marks made
by a double-paneled revolving door; bits of lead still remain in the traces of its hinges. This staircase is pictured
on page 183 and can also be located on Site Plan B,
page 178.

Marinatos would seldom relax his ironclad rule about
excavating. His teams were forbidden to use any method
that placed them in physical danger or caused further
damage to a ruin. *This was a living museum.* When a buried building could be reached only by tunneling, its excavation was restricted indefinitely to the upper floors.

The early 1970s were years of great discoveries. Teams
of engineers and technicians worked simultaneously at
different projects in various parts of the south sectors.
Some were assigned to brace weak ruins as the first stage
in the long process of restoration. Until they were made
safe, more complete excavation was not attempted. The
ancient buildings had been subjected to unthinkable
stresses, from earthquake shocks to bombardment by
showers of fiery volcanic rocks that tore gaping holes in
their walls. The slight submergence of the earth left them
weirdly deformed.

From this time on, the various teams were routinely
working as deep as twenty-five and thirty feet below
ground level. The lowest layer of volcanic debris was a
thick white bank of pumice in which many, but not all
buildings, were buried.

As quickly as they were found, the protective shed was
extended to cover them. Its roof and sides were fitted with

View of Delta sector showing depth of excavation. (Photograph by Mary Alice Keir.)

translucent panels and admitted daylight. Work was not held up as in former years by bad weather. A wall along the eastern boundary of the site supported one end of the shed. At its base is the underground concrete channel by which the winter runoff of the torrent is diverted. A stout fence encloses the site on its other three sides.

Engineers and technicians were always on the watch for telltale impressions in the ash. These were the "prints" left by disintegrated beams, windowsills, and other parts of a building's original framework. The hollow impressions were filled with reinforced concrete or plaster of Paris. As it set, it retained the shape of the evaporated

Partial restoration of the Spring Fresco Room, Delta 2. The window frame is reconstructed. (Photograph by Mary Alice Keir.)

wood. In the last stage of restoration, the plaster of Paris shape was often copied in olive wood because this is what had served the Minoan carpenters. Every excavated or partly excavated building represented a heavy investment of skilled labor and sophisticated technical know-how.

Little could match the tense excitement of moments when frescoes were discovered in long-buried rooms. Each decision about saving them was made by a committee of art restorers and technicians. The now famous "Spring Fresco" was found in Delta 2, a small room known also as "The Lilies Room." A mixture of ash and sand filled it. During its removal several bright red lilies became visible

Partial restoration the Spring Fresco Room of Delta 2. The window frame is reconstructed. (Photograph by Mary Alice Keir.)

on one wall. In a matter of minutes, lilies began to show up on two other walls.

The staff specialist in restoration took over the delicate job of cleaning the three plaster panels of hardened ash. While he was working, as if by magic a continuous landscape reappeared. On all three walls playful swallows could be seen darting and soaring above sharp, rocky cliffs where clusters of bright red lilies bloom.

With some regret Marinatos agreed that the entire fresco—three large panels—should be removed from the site. An Athens museum had the finest facilities for restoring a magnificent prehistoric painting. The plaster panels were covered with gauze strips to hold in place any cracked or swollen parts. Each one was then successfully

The Spring Fresco Room, restored, in National Museum of Athens. (Copyright 1971 Smithsonian Institution. Photograph by Dimitri Kessel.)

detached from its wall and the three were shipped to Athens in special wooden crates.

The nameless painter of this colorful springtime scene displayed an understanding of perspective in his handling of the birds in flight. He was easily a thousand years ahead of his Greek successors in this bold achievement. Several details of the Spring Fresco appear on page 192.

The technicians noticed a number of irregular impressions in the ash layer remaining on the floor of Delta 2. More prints! They used a process first perfected at Pompeii to fill the irregular hollows with gypsum. After it hardened and underwent further treatment, they were elated to recover the "cast" or mold of a wooden bed. It came out complete, with legs and sides intact and the crisp imprint

Detail of swallows from the Spring Fresco. (Copyright 1971 Smithsonian Institution. Photograph by Dimitri Kessel.)

Detail of lilies from the Spring Fresco. (Copyright 1971 Smithsonian Institution. Photograph by Dimitri Kessel.)

of thin ropes that supported an animal skin or some sort of fabric as its mattress. The impressions literally *gave back* the original forms of these objects. Furniture makers have produced an exact replica of the bed and of a wooden stool that stood near it.

These were not the last of the treasures in Delta 2. There was a collection of goblets and vases, many of bronze, so good in design that Marinatos described them as "noble." Cooking vessels included bronze frying pans much like those Theran women cook with today. One was engraved with the sign of the sacred double axe, signifying that it was for use only in religious rites. Everything about The Lilies Room, particularly the quality of its hoard of vases, suggested that it had been a shrine. The presence of the bed hinted that some squatter might have lived here, surrounded by things of value he hoped to save, until he was driven out by the horrifying explosions of the volcano.

Another discovery of 1970 was "The Boxing Boys" fresco, page 194. These serious young fellows were found on one wall of B1 when its lower floor was cleared. The other walls held paintings of graceful antelopes. Only a single panel of these could be removed for restoration; the others were too badly broken and defaced. The "survivor" is shown on page 195.

Art historians judge the frescoes of the spring landscape, the boxers, and the antelopes to be the finest prehistoric paintings yet found in the Mediterranean area. Thera's painters had attained a high level of artistry in the sixteenth century B.C. Their work is vigorous and free, not yet so stylized as the first Minoan frescoes found at Knossos. Who the Theran painters were may forever be a secret, nor is it known whether they lived on the island or were freelance artists from other Minoan cities.

The red boxing gloves worn by the children are the earliest ever pictured. It is uncertain whether each child has on one glove or two because many fragments of the panel could not be found. The boys wear their long hair in Minoan style and their heads are covered with tight-fitting blue caps. The royal blue color is thought to mean that they are young princes. Again, however, no one knows.

Like the swallows of the Spring Fresco, the antelopes are so lifelike that their species was quickly identified. They raise an interesting question. This antelope now is native to East Africa. Was the painter recreating some-

thing he had seen there, perhaps as a traveler, or could
the animal be found on ancient Thera?

Delta sector held a multitude of surprises. The excavators came upon two kinds of inlaid floors. One consisted
of several layers of tamped earth. Colorful small sea pebbles had been pounded into the topmost layer. The other
type of earthen floor had a top layer of powdered snail
and sea shells. Even now, as one of them was swept clean
with a fine brush, it glinted faintly with its once bright

The Boxing Boys Fresco, from Room Beta 1. (Copyright 1971
Smithsonian Institution. Photograph by Dimitri Kessel.)

mother-of-pearl luster. One can believe that these were
the forerunners of the beautiful mosaic floors popular in
the homes of prosperous Greek citizens and later in Roman houses. At Thera they were pretty variations on the
slab flooring found in other rooms.

Any account of the Thera excavations that dwells on
spectacular discoveries but slights the less dramatic findings cannot do justice to a large group of talented people.
With smoothly coordinated teamwork they were recover-

The Antelopes Fresco, from Room Beta 1. (Copyright 1971
Smithsonian Institution. Photograph by Dimitri Kessel.)

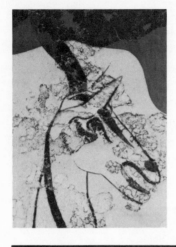

Detail of Antelopes Fresco.
(Copyright 1971
Smithsonian Institution.
Photograph by Dimitri Kessel.)

---

ing the contents of many a ruined building, not just the building alone. Staff members dismissed nothing as unimportant. Everything, ranging from broken shards of kitchen pots to the brilliant paintings on Theran walls, has meaning. All the items found, ordinary and extraordinary alike, are the "prints" of human lives. The people who left them were lost for centuries to time and history. It is tempting to think that their courtesy title "Minoan" may someday be replaced with their rightful name, which unexpectedly reveals itself in a few lines of that writing known as Linear A, scratched on the side of a mud brick or cut into the clay of a vase. The thought, however, is pure fantasy.

But was theirs the city and Thera the island that Plato decided to call Atlantis? From the evidence now at hand, there seems good reason to think they could have been. This is a statement of fact, not a fantasy.

XXVI

A Goal Is Attained

 The pattern of buildings and courtyards in the south end of the site was becoming so clearly defined that a pathway for visitors was opened in 1973. Since the 1970 season, Xesté 3 and other large buildings had been excavated. With work continuing in other sectors as well, two more courtyards were cleared. The area under protective roofing now covered nearly twelve acres.

The south sectors had taken on the semblance of a pleasant neighborhood in a "live" city. It had an atmosphere of its own. Every now and then tourists could be heard wondering where "the people who live here" had gone and when they might suddenly return. Staff members certainly understood that feeling. The subdued light under the shed made the ruins appear a pale gray-white or sometimes a faint yellow color. Even the fine dust stirred up by visitors' feet was the powdery drift of volcanic ash. It was a place at once real and unreal.

The pathway marked the attainment of a major goal. People arriving at the site entered *a living museum* where they could walk among the once-buried buildings of a Minoan city and see them at close range. Groups of visitors were led by guides, some of whom had worked on the dig for years. The entrance was at the south end of the site, in sector Gamma.

Xesté 3 was the first large structure on their left as the pathway took them north under the great shed. Twelve ground-floor rooms had been opened in this building. An impressive double stairway led to the first floor, and parts of this were quite well preserved. Frescoes of women

General view of the covered site, 1979, looking toward Akrotiri. (Photograph by C. Shutes.)

gathering spring flowers decorated several walls. Plan B shows the site as it was in 1973. The route taken by visitors can be followed by referring to the Plan.

During its excavation no evidence was found to indicate that Xesté 3 had been a private residence. Instead, it seemed designed for use by large groups of people. Near each of its two entrances was a built-in stone bench for a doorkeeper, and each door opened into an anteroom where stone benches lined the walls. Marinatos thought they were for workers and artisans who waited their turns to receive food supplies as payment for their labor. A city as large as this would require an efficient system of administration.

As they continued northward, visitors were walking on the cobblestones of Telchines Road. It began to widen out on the approach to the first courtyard. Through restored window and door frames people could see the interiors of storerooms and workshops. Most buildings were preserved to the level of their second storeys and were from twenty to twenty-five feet high. Their upper floors and roofs had collapsed before or during the final catastrophe. There were rare exceptions: a few second-floor rooms had been reconstructed. The west wing of a second floor was partly restored in one mansion.

Massive banks of volcanic matter still awaited removal in several places. These were layers of pumice and ash mixed with sand and pebbles. Anyone who knew Thera's tragic history could recognize them for what they were. Marinatos described one of the strata as "the catastrophe layer" because it contained traces of an earlier settlement underlying Alpha and Delta sectors. An earthquake had destroyed it fifty to seventy years before the eruption.

When the town was rebuilt, parts of new buildings were constructed with materials salvaged from the old. Walls that remained upright were made to support or strengthen new walls. Sir Arthur Evans had encountered similar conditions at Knossos, and now the Thera excavations were yielding fresh evidence that both islands had shared the sequence of disasters: the two earthquakes and the eruption. Crete suffered grievously from its aftermath, but the impact of the eruption on Thera was immediate.

The catastrophe layer accounted for a host of puzzling architectural elements. Besides explaining the presence of double walls and very old fresco fragments behind later paintings, it revealed that the great complex known as Xesté 1 had undergone innumerable building phases. Like Xesté 3, it seemed intended for the use of many persons. Only rooms Beta 1 through 8 could be singled out as private residential quarters. To mark the distinction more clearly, the term *Xesté 1* was now used less often than the more exact "Building Complex Beta" and "Building Complex Delta." Visitors on Telchines Road passed close to them as their guides pointed out various rooms in which the famous Spring Fresco, the Boxing Boys, and other wall paintings had been found.

The on-going excavations had also brought logical changes in the names assigned to one courtyard and several buildings. The first open-air plaza to be excavated was called North Court for a time, but it more appropriately became Millhouse Square when another complete mill was found in room Delta 15. In it were millstones, a stone workbench, and a large vat for catching flour while it was being ground. From the pathway people could see these objects clearly, everything left exactly as it had been uncovered. The photo on this page gives a visitor's-eye view of the millroom, seen from the south.

As they left Millhouse Square, just ahead of them was one of the most distinctive buildings of the site. This was the Pylon, a high, monumental gate with two side entrances. In form it was a pyramid without an apex, jutting out protectively from the western entrance of Building Complex Delta. Tourists could walk through its side entrances and continue on their way toward the second courtyard.

Again the road widened and they were in Triangle Court, so named because of its shape. On their right was the Polythyron, a rather mysterious apartment consisting of rooms Delta 1 and 1a on the first floor. *Polythyron*

The Millhouse in Delta sector. View of the entrance as one approaches from the south. (Photograph by Mary Alice Keir.)

means "room of many doors," and it was exactly that. Its two rooms were separated by a wall in which there had been a row of five interconnecting doors. Their posts were still in place. Marinatos believed that it had been a shrine or cult room for religious rites. His judgment took into consideration the sorts of pottery and rare ceremonial objects found inside. The ground floor apparently was a storeroom, filled as it was with many large jars.

The third courtyard was at the far north end of Building Complex Delta. Right there, close to the western wall, the digging crew had gently removed the fossilized branches of a little tree. Someone had built a low, semicircular stone fence at its base to protect the young trunk. Decorated flowerpots with drainage holes were fairly common finds, but this was the first hint of an ancient garden within the city. As visitors moved through the courtyard they were beginning to realize that each of these open plazas must have been an inviting place for people to gather on warm summer evenings, to greet friends and enjoy the cooling sea air.

Even by modern standards this was a planned community. Courtyards served the same purpose that parks do in cities and towns today. They were not overshadowed by the boldly designed public buildings and private mansions. While the plan undoubtedly evolved over a long period of time, it could not be by accident that provision was made for the comfort and convenience of the townspeople.

The ruins in Alpha sector were the next point of interest as visitors proceeded to the north end of the site. The three-part storeroom had been completely excavated, though serious damage had been done by winter flooding

Door and window of the House of the Fishermen, over-looking Triangle Square. (Photograph by Mary Alice Keir.)

before the torrent was channeled. Its ground floor was literally crammed with huge jars of different shapes and sizes. Some contained carbonized seeds and grains. The first millroom discovered was part of this group, which now was called Building Complex Alpha.

It was here that the pathway reversed its direction and visitors turned southward to begin the return walk. A short distance to the southwest of the storeroom, guides stopped to call attention to the building known as House of the Ladies, another mansion that originally had been three storeys tall. Frescoes of graceful and beautifully dressed Minoan women were found on the walls of its second storey. They are considered to be among the most handsome of Thera's paintings. Marinatos suggested that, like the frescoes of women gathering spring flowers in Xesté 3, they were meant to represent goddesses or women of royalty in a religious ceremony that celebrated the coming of spring.

The mansion discovered early in the 1967 season faced Triangle Square across from the Polythyron. After its excavation in 1972 the name West House was no longer suitable, and it became House of the Fisherman when frescoes were found of two men, two-thirds life size, holding strings of newly caught fish. After long preparation most of the west wing of its second storey was successfully restored. It included a bedroom distinguished as much for its plan as for its unusual frescoes, which identified the owner as a man of high naval rank and importance. The walls were decorated with flaglike banners called *ikria,* the symbols of Minoan sea power. Later studies suggest that they represented the raised deck chair used on shipboard by the commanding officer. The chair was enclosed with a tentlike canopy on which ikria designs were painted.

One discovery truly amazed the excavators. Adjoining the bedroom they found a complete bathroom with a toilet: two stone slabs with a slit between them. No indoor toilet—and on the second floor, at that—had been known to exist in a building of such age. The bathtub lay where it had fallen through to the first floor. Even a three-legged bronze cauldron was recovered; it could have heated water for the bath. Clay drainpipes in one wall carried waste from the second-floor lavatory to an underground, stone-lined pit that also served a nearby building.

The frescoes throughout House of the Fisherman were unlike any found on Thera or at other Minoan sites. The so-called Miniature Fresco was discovered in another second-floor room. Marinatos said that it was ". . . perhaps destined to open a new chapter in the history of the Aegean." No archaeologist or naval historian has disagreed with him. Its center of interest is a flotilla of Minoan ships of the sixteenth century B.C. No one had known what they looked like. This is the first contemporary painting of ships to be found. (The reconstruction of one ship is on page 206.)

What remained of the fresco measured seven feet in length and was only eight inches high. It formed a continuous band across the two walls that could be restored. The other two walls had been destroyed. Multicolored fragments on the floor indicated that the fresco had extended across all four walls.

Marinatos and his coworkers were sadly familiar with the destructiveness of volcanic activity, but nowhere was its power more starkly evident than in this ruined house.

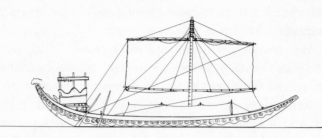

A Minoan ship, one of those in the Miniature Fresco in the House of the Fisherman, adapted from the fresco by Thomas C. Gillmer. (Photograph courtesy of Prof. Thomas C. Gillmer. Reprinted with permission of *The Mariner's Mirror*.)

Scientists use the term "base surge" to describe the first phase of a nuclear bomb explosion, when a mushroom-shaped cloud rolls outward and upward from the ground. Hot winds of hurricane force are instantly generated. Volcanologists have observed the same base surge effect during the earliest stage of a great eruption. In House of the Fisherman the paintings on walls that faced windows opposite the exploding crater looked as if they had been struck by pellets fired from a shotgun. Fresco sections that could be recovered and restored were on interior walls and had been somewhat sheltered from the violent winds and airborne particles of sand.

In the fresco seven ships at sea are either approaching or leaving one of three small towns and are escorted by leaping dolphins. Originally there must have been more than twenty ships, all equipped with square sails, and many with banks of oarsmen and paddlers. Important-looking passengers are seen on some ships; they are not in military dress. Townspeople stand on the roofs of buildings at the water's edge as the ships pass in parade formation. A naval battle may have occurred, for injured and dying sailors float helplessly in the water. Other scenes show a mountainous landscape filled with wild animals and birds. Sheep and goats with their herdsmen roam on wooded hillsides.

Above all, it is the ships that command attention. The artist's concern with fine details enables naval historians to estimate their sizes—from eighty to one hundred feet in length—and to study their construction. One may be the flagship; the figure of a crouched lion is draped over its stern. Similar animal devices seem to show the ranks of other ships. Just behind the helmsman on the flagship is a small canopied deck house—an ikrion. It happens that the design on its canopy is identical to those on the bedroom walls in House of the Fisherman, where it is repeated eight times. Can one doubt that the commander of the flagship was also the owner of the mansion? Was he perhaps the admiral of the fleet?

The regional backgrounds of the various scenes are a series of unsolved puzzles. If Thera is the setting for some of them, it isn't clear what region of the ancient world is the background for others. In one section a river courses through a rocky desert. Its banks are lined with tropical palm trees, and lions pursue terrified deer. Is it meant to be somewhere in Libya, on the North African coast? Minoan townspeople, sailors, and armor-clad soldiers can be recognized among the dozens of tiny human figures. Others wear strange garments like long fur coats and offer another historical mystery. That so much of the Miniature Fresco survived for modern eyes to see is something of a miracle. One understands why Marinatos affectionately called it a *precious* find.

General view of Gamma sector from the southwest,

Building Gamma was on the visitors' right as they walked south, back to the point where they had entered the site. Because many anvils, hammerstones, and grindstones were found in its rooms, it is thought that the squatters stored their tools here when they weren't using them to demolish walls weakened by earth shocks. But their struggle to keep alive in that harsh interval between earthquake and eruption was abruptly halted. The last survivors were driven away forever.

looking toward North Court. (Photograph by Mary Alice Keir.)

The path taken by visitors is by no means a fixed and permanent walkway. Its course has already been altered several times as additional ruins became accessible to visitors. Archaeologists estimate that it will take a hundred years to reclaim the rest of Thera's buried city. In keeping with the living museum concept, the pathway can be expected to undergo many changes, always reflecting the growth and expansion of the site itself.

XXVII

After Six Seasons

🌿 What started as an exploratory dig in a dusty ravine had become, in only five years, a major archaeological undertaking. The ever-expanding shed enclosed buildings and streets that once were the harbor section of a Minoan city. Some ruins were beautifully restored, others in various stages of excavation.

Were they the ruins of Atlantis?

Whenever the question was put to him, Dr. Marinatos was cautious. It bored him. Surely he had made his position unmistakably clear in 1967 and after that in many articles and interviews. He could only repeat—endlessly, it seemed—that Atlantis was a side issue, a separate problem.

His purpose at Thera was to prove the correctness of his theory about the ancient eruption. Late in the sixteenth century B.C. it tore the island apart, leaving it barren and uninhabited. Earthquakes, fires, and deposits of volcanic waste caused the palaces of Crete to be abandoned, with Knossos the last to be deserted. The Minoans could not recover from the loss of their ships, their crops, and even their cities. How many human lives were lost will never be known. Gradually the Mycenaeans of mainland Greece rose to power as the dominant political authority. The brilliant Minoan civilization was brought to its end by the terrible consequences of Thera's eruption.

His reconstruction of these events first took shape while Marinatos was excavating on Crete nearly forty years earlier. The accuracy of his theory was being dramatically confirmed: the site was yielding massive amounts of evidence about the exact nature and the magnitude of the disaster.

Regardless of anything Marinatos said or wrote, the argument that Thera was Plato's lost Atlantis went merrily on. Those who did not understand what the excavations had already revealed could be misled into thinking that the Atlantis connection was more important than the discoveries themselves. The whole thing was a distraction. Marinatos was tired of it.

Then, in 1969, he went to the trouble of releasing the English version of a paper he first published in 1950, at that time only in Greek. Its title was "A Few Words About the Legend of Atlantis." In a new preface he said it had become apparent to him ". . . that sooner or later the Atlantis question would warm up again. . . ." The matter had actually come to a boil. He obviously wanted to reach an international audience and set Atlantis in proper perspective once and for all.

Because the eruption submerged parts of Thera, he

wrote, it could well be ". . . the historical core of a legend . . . the raison d'être [the very reason for being] of the Atlantis literature." Lost or sunken lands were traditions in many cultures, including those of Egypt and India, to name only two. But Atlantis represented a special Aegean tradition, and he called Plato its "bearer." The core of that legend can be accepted as authentic history, but assuredly not the place or the time Plato assigned to it.

He explained that both errors can be understood by searching out the historical elements of the legend and separating them from other elements of fantasy and distortion which combined to create it.

The explosion of Thera is its core. The Egyptians were aware that some catastrophe had overwhelmed a powerful, wealthy island to the west, causing it to sink and killing thousands of people. They assumed that Crete was the island when the traders they called "the men of Keftiu," or Cretans, mysteriously disappeared from the seas they had controlled. It is possible that the Egyptians knew little or nothing about Thera, either that it existed or that much of it had been destroyed. For generations the Atlantis legend derived its strength from rumors and word-of-mouth stories, which grew with the telling. The deaths of thousands of people were finally attributed to a war, and those who died were "soldiers."

Long before the lifetime of Solon or of Plato, then, the legend was a fusion of real events and mistaken interpretations of them. Even so, it embodied certain faint outlines of Plato's tale. Marinatos noted that there is no way to tell whether that story had its origin in Egypt or was wholly Plato's invention. Solon's journey to Egypt, some-

time after 572 B.C., is a well-documented fact; he could
very well have heard it from Egyptian priests.

One other event probably reinforced the idea that the
stricken island was located in the Atlantic Ocean. Marinatos pointed out that in the sixth century B.C., a thousand
years after Thera's eruption, the Egyptian Pharaoh Necho
commissioned a Phoenician ship to circumnavigate the
continent of Africa, a three-year voyage. The route they
took was northward, along Africa's west coast. That route
and the "wonderful tales" told by the returning sailors
about what they saw in the Mediterranean and Aegean
Seas helped to fix Atlantis in its traditional location. "The
most recent elements of the myth descend to about 600
B.C. Nine hundred years have thus been covered." It was a
strange mix of fantasy and fact, which the Egyptian priest
". . . projected tenfold into the abyss of the past. It thus
reached, together with so much else that was impossible,
the impossible chronology of nine thousand years before
Solon's era."

This vigorous summing-up of his position reveals Marinatos at his best. He draws on his knowledge of Egyptian
literature and history to compare two thousand years of
events in Egypt's past with what is now known about the
same period for the Minoans and Mycenaeans. He uses
the recorded events of written history to explain the errors
of place and time in Plato's account of Atlantis. These
have always been two of its most puzzling aspects.

His attitude toward the legend was thoroughly consistent. With every mention of it he called it the Atlantis
problem or the Atlantis *question,* as though to deprive it
of its undeserved glamour and lay it to rest forever. The
nineteenth century had Ignatius Donnelly as a champion

of the romantic Atlantis. In the twentieth, Spyridon Marinatos was its unrelenting foe.

The article was his last official comment on the subject. Dr. Marinatos had spent six seasons at Akrotiri, chal-
lenged by the incredible complexities of the work, elated
by every find that provided new information about the
way the people of Thera lived. After each season he wrote
and published an annual report on the progress of the
excavations.

He announced his retirement in 1973. And in October,
1974, when he was less than a month from his seventy-
third birthday, he returned to the site. As he stood on an
embankment giving directions to a workman a short distance below, he slipped, lost his balance, and fell. He died
instantly of a fractured skull. It was an ironic way for this
man to meet death. He took pride in the fact that since
1967 there had been only one fatal accident on the site.
A crewman was killed in 1970 while helping to put up
an extension of the shed. Otherwise the safety record was
unblemished.

Marinatos was buried on the site. It had become a
living museum, as he had intended and planned. It is his
best memorial. He also trained two generations of Greek
archaeologists in the years he taught at the University of
Athens, beginning in 1939. The list of his honors and
awards, like that of his writings, is long. The "mysterious
Minoans," as they were often described, are no longer
quite so mysterious, thanks to his years in field archaeology
and research.

Dr. Christos Doumas had worked with him as his as-
sistant since 1971 and was named to succeed Marinatos
as director of the excavation. He, too, was an archaeologist
of broad experience.

Some digging continued in the south sector, but after the strenuous labor and excitement of six busy seasons, it was on a much reduced scale. Sections of the enclosed areas had been set aside as storage compartments for the vast collection of unclassified finds that accumulated from season to season. It was decided to give them the attention they required. The site entered a new phase of evaluation and study as Dr. Doumas and his staff turned their attention to these tasks.

A total of thirty buildings had been uncovered since the first dig in 1967. By 1976, twelve frescoes in all had been restored. It can be misleading to cite numbers, however. No two buildings, large or small, were similar in design or construction. All had been affected by volcanic activity and earthquakes.

The Thera excavations might be compared to the restoration of one gigantic fresco from thousands upon thousands of splintered, scattered fragments. On several occasions Marinatos said that the work of rescuing the remains of the ruined town could take a hundred years.

As long as Thera is an active site, there will be no lack of interest in what archaeologists discover there. Any significant find or finds will revive the theories that connect the island with Plato's lost Atlantis. And the legend may very well go on growing. Assuredly, the arguments will do the same.

BIBLIOGRAPHY

Alsop, Joseph Wright. FROM THE SILENT EARTH; A REPORT ON THE GREEK BRONZE AGE. New York: Harper & Row, 1964.

Bramwell, James Guy. LOST ATLANTIS. New York: Harper, 1938.

Burland, Cottie Arthur. THE GODS OF MEXICO. New York: G.P. Putnam's Sons, 1967.

Carpenter, Rhys. BEYOND THE PILLARS OF HERCULES. New York: Dial Press, 1966.

————. DISCONTINUITY IN GREEK CIVILIZATION. New York: Cambridge University Press, 1966.

Cary, Max and T.J. Haarhoff. LIFE AND THOUGHT IN THE GREEK AND ROMAN WORLD. London: Methuen and Co., 1957.

Chapin, Henry. THE SEARCH FOR ATLANTIS. New York: Macmillan, 1968.

Churchward, James. THE CHILDREN OF MU. New York: Ives Washburn, 1938.

De Camp, Lyon Sprague. LOST CONTINENTS; THE ATLANTIS THEME IN HISTORY, SCIENCE, AND LITERATURE. New York: Gnome Press, Inc., 1954.

De Selincourt, Aubrey. THE WORLD OF HERODOTUS. Boston: Little, Brown and Co., 1962.

Donnelly, Ignatius. ATLANTIS: THE ANTEDILUVIAN WORLD. A modern revised edition edited by Egerton Sykes. New York: Harper and Brothers, 1949.

Doumas, Christos. SANTORIN. Milan: Publications Delta, 1977.

Evans, Joan. TIME AND CHANCE; THE STORY OF ARTHUR EVANS. London: Longmans, Green and Co., 1943.

Fouqué, Ferdinand. SANTORIN ET SES ÉRUPTIONS. Edited by G. Masson. Paris: Libraire de l'Académe de Medecine, 1879.

Frost, K.T. "The *Critias* and Minoan Crete," JOURNAL OF HELLENIC STUDIES, XXXIII (1913), 189–206.

Galanapoulos, Angelos Georgiou and Edward Bacon. ATLANTIS; THE TRUTH BEHIND THE LEGEND. Indianapolis: Bobbs-Merrill Co., 1969.

Gillmer, Thomas C. "Ships of Atlantis," SEA FRONTIERS, XXI. No. 6 (November–December, 1975), 351–358.

———: "The Thera Ship," THE MARINER'S MIRROR, LXI, No. 4 (November, 1975), 321–329.

Graham, James Walter. THE PALACES OF CRETE. Princeton, N.J.: Princeton University Press, 1962.

Hale, John Rigby and the Editors of Time-Life Books. THE AGE OF EXPLORATION. New York: Time, Inc., 1966.

Heezen, Bruce C. "A Time Clock for History." SATURDAY REVIEW, Dec. 6, 1969, 87–90.

Holbrook, Stewart Hall. LOST MEN OF AMERICAN HISTORY. New York: Macmillan, 1947.

Horwitz, Sylvia L., THE FIND OF A LIFETIME. SIR ARTHUR EVANS AND THE DISCOVERY OF KNOSSOS. New York: The Viking Press, 1981.

Johnson, Gerald White. THE LUNATIC FRINGE. New York: J.P. Lippincott Co., 1957.

Luce, John Victor. LOST ATLANTIS: NEW LIGHT ON AN OLD LEGEND. New York: McGraw-Hill, 1969.

Mamet, Henri. DE INSULA THERA. Paris: Thorin, 1874.

Marinatos, Spyridon. CRETE AND MYCENAE. New York: Harry N. Abrams, Inc., 1960.

———. EXCAVATIONS AT THERA, FIRST PRELIMINARY REPORT (1967 SEASON). Athens: Archaeological Society of Athens, 1968.

———. EXCAVATIONS AT THERA II (1968 SEASON). Athens: Archaeological Society of Athens, 1969.

———. EXCAVATIONS AT THERA III (1969 SEASON). Athens: Archaeological Society of Athens, 1970.

———. EXCAVATIONS AT THERA IV (1970 SEASON). Athens: Archaeological Society of Athens, 1971.

———. EXCAVATIONS AT THERA V (1971 SEASON). Athens: Archaeological Society of Athens, 1972.

———. EXCAVATIONS AT THERA VI (1972 SEASON). Athens: Archaeological Society of Athens, 1974.

———. EXCAVATIONS AT THERA VII (1973 SEASON). Athens: Archaeological Society of Athens, 1976.

———. "Life and Art in Prehistoric Thera," PROCEEDINGS OF THE BRITISH ACADEMY, LVII. London: Oxford University Press, 1972.

————. "Some Words about the Legend of Atlantis."
Archailogicon Deltion No. 12 (Athens), 1969. Second
edition, 1971.

————. "Thera: Key to the Riddle of Minos," NATIONAL
GEOGRAPHIC, CXLI, No. 5 (May, 1972), 702–726.

————. "The Volcanic Destruction of Minoan Crete,"
ANTIQUITY, XIII (December, 1939), 425–439.

Mavor, James Watt, Jr. VOYAGE TO ATLANTIS. New York:
Putnam's, 1969.

Morison, Samuel Eliot. THE EUROPEAN DISCOVERY OF AMERICA:
THE NORTHERN VOYAGES, A.D. 500–1600. New York:
Oxford University Press, 1971.

Morley, Sylvanus Griswold. THE ANCIENT MAYA. 3d ed., revised,
by George W. Brainerd. Stanford, Calif.: Stanford University
Press, 1956.

Morse, Robert. "The Frescoes of Thera; Spectacular Finds in
Ancient Aegean Rubble," SMITHSONIAN, II, No. 10
(January, 1972), 15–23.

Outhwaite, Leonard. UNROLLING THE MAP: THE STORY OF
EXPLORATION. New York: Reynal and Hitchcock, 1935.

Page, Denys L. THE SANTORINI VOLCANO AND THE DESOLATION
OF MINOAN CRETE. (Supplementary Paper No. 12).
London: The Society for the Promotion of Hellenic Studies,
1970.

Prescott, William Hickling. THE CONQUEST OF MEXICO. London:
J.M. Dent and Sons, Ltd., 1957.

Roberts, Cokie and Steven V. "Atlantis Recaptured," NEW YORK
TIMES MAGAZINE (September 5, 1976), 12–13; 34–37.

Spence, Lewis. ATLANTIS IN AMERICA. New York: Brentano's,
1925.

————. HISTORY OF ATLANTIS. Philadelphia: McKay, 1927.

————. THE PROBLEM OF ATLANTIS. New York: Brentano's,
1924.

————. THE PROBLEM OF LEMURIA, THE SUNKEN CONTINENT
OF THE PACIFIC. Philadelphia: McKay, 1933.

Stephens, John Lloyd. INCIDENTS OF TRAVEL IN YUCATÁN.
Edited by Victor Wolfgang von Hagen. Norman, Okla.:
University of Oklahoma Press, 1962.

Thompson, John Eric Sidney. A COMMENTARY ON THE DRESDEN
    CODEX: A MAYA HIEROGLYPHIC BOOK. Philadelphia:
    American Philosophical Society, 1972.

————. THE RISE AND FALL OF MAYA CIVILIZATION. Norman,
    Okla.: University of Oklahoma Press, 1954.

Tozzer, Alfred M., ed. LANDA'S RELACIÓN DE LAS COSAS DE
    YUCATÁN. A TRANSLATION. (Papers of the Peabody
    Museum of American Archaeology and Ethnology, XVIII,
    Harvard University, 1941.)

Vermeule, Emily Townsend. GREECE IN THE BRONZE AGE.
    Chicago: University of Chicago Press, 1964.

————. "The Promise of Thera," ATLANTIC, CCXX, No. 6
    (December, 1967), 83–94.

Vitaliano, Dorothy B. LEGENDS OF THE EARTH: THEIR
    GEOLOGICAL ORIGINS. Bloomington, Ind.: Indiana University
    Press, 1973.

Von Hagen, Victor Wolfgang. THE ANCIENT SUN KINGDOMS OF
    THE AMERICAS. New York: World Publishing Co., 1961.

————. MAYA EXPLORER; JOHN LLOYD STEPHENS AND THE
    LOST CITIES OF CENTRAL AMERICA AND YUCATÁN.
    Norman, Okla.: University of Oklahoma Press, 1947.

————. SEARCH FOR THE MAYA: THE STORY OF STEPHENS AND
    CATHERWOOD. Farnborough, England: Saxon House,
    D.C. Heath, Ltd., 1973.

Wauchope, Robert. LOST TRIBES AND SUNKEN CONTINENTS:
    MYTH AND METHOD IN THE STUDY OF AMERICAN INDIANS.
    Chicago: University of Chicago Press, 1962.

INDEX

(Illustrations are indicated by **bold face** *entries)*